MACMILLAN CARIBBEAN DIVE GUIDES

Trinidad & Tobago

Solomon Baksh

Series Editor: Sandra Baksh

MACMILLAN
CARIBBEAN

D0932252

Macmillan Education
Between Towns Road, Oxford OX4 3PP
A division of Macmillan Publishers Limited
Companies and representatives throughout the world

www.macmillan-caribbean.com

ISBN 1-405-01336-2

Text © Solomon Baksh 2005
Design and illustration © Macmillan Publishers Limited 2005

First published 2005

All rights reserved; no part of this publication may be
reproduced, stored in a retrieval system, transmitted in any
form or by any means, electronic, mechanical, photocopying,
recording, or otherwise, without the prior written permission
of the publishers.

Designed by Solomon Baksh
Typeset by Solomon Baksh and Carol Hulme
Maps by Tek-Art
Photographs by Solomon Baksh except page 22, (bottom):
Kirwin Sampson/Keisha Sandy
Cover design by Bob Swan
Cover photographs by Solomon Baksh

Printed and bound in Thailand

2009 2008 2007 2006 2005
10 9 8 7 6 5 4 3 2 1

CONTENTS

ACKNOWLEDGEMENTS

This dive guide would not have been possible without the support and help of some treasured people – my wife Sandy whose literary skills, technical input and research were invaluable; Gerry Chun Taite my dear friend, dive buddy and super cook, who introduced me to the wonders of scuba diving so many years ago; Amsie Baksh and Jose Sanchez; Andre Fraser, Ostra Trotman and Marvin Phillips, my dive buddies in Tobago; Rikky Knowles and Rae de Beer of World of Watersports; Kevin Frank, the most knowledgable diver about Speyside diving; Carole, Anne and Bjarne who are all far away but fondly remembered; John and Wendy Austin, Tracy Kearns and Jackie of R & Sea Divers Limited; Marcus Baumgarten of Extra Divers; Goran and Amanda Qvarfort of Manta Dive Center; Sean Robinson and his staff of Tobago Dive Experience; the staff of Manta Lodge in Speyside; Kirwin Sampson and Keisha Sandy of DMRF, Tobago House of Assembly.

Divers exploring one of the numerous overhangs at Cove Ledge

INTRODUCTION

Location

Trinidad and Tobago are the most southern of the Caribbean islands. Located just 7 miles off the eastern coast of Venezuela, Trinidad is at the mouth of the Orinoco River and is separated from the mainland by the Gulf of Paria. This twin-island, English-speaking, republic offers contrasts in lifestyle, activities, culture and natural resources. Tobago is just off the north-eastern tip of Trinidad and is only about 21 miles (33 km) from its nearest point at Toco.

Trinidad is the larger, more industrialised island, with an area of 1,864 sq miles (4,828 sq km). Tobago is much smaller and is tourism-driven, with an area of 116 sq miles (300 sq km).

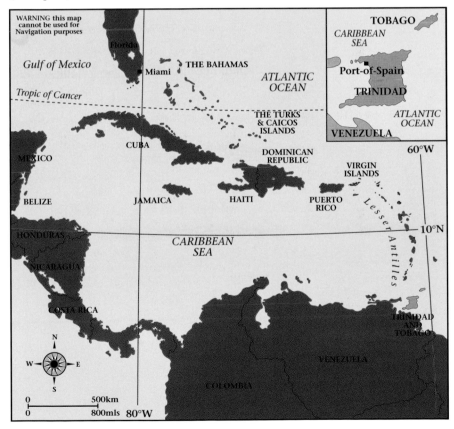

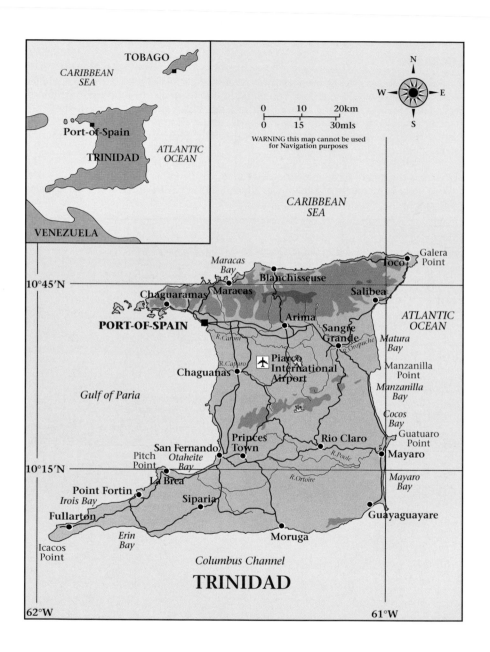

TOBAGO

CARIBBEAN
SEA

N
W — E
S

Port-of-Spain

TRINIDAD

ATLANTIC
OCEAN

VENEZUELA

0   10   20km
0   15   30mls

WARNING this map cannot be used
for Navigation purposes

CARIBBEAN
SEA

Galera
Point

Maracas
Bay

Toco

10°45′N

Blanchisseuse

Salibea

Chaguaramas Maracas

PORT-OF-SPAIN

ATLANTIC
OCEAN

Arima

Sangre
Grande

Matura
Bay

R.Caroni

Piarco
International
Airport

R.Oropuche

Chaguanas

R.Caparo

Manzanilla
Point

Gulf of Paria

Manzanilla
Bay

Cocos
Bay

Princes
Town

Rio Claro

Guatuaro
Point

San Fernando

Mayaro

Pitch
Point

Otaheite
Bay

R.Poole

10°15′N

R.Ortoire

Mayaro
Bay

Point Fortin

La Brea

Irois Bay

Siparia

Fullarton

Guayaguayare

Erin
Bay

Icacos
Point

Moruga

Columbus Channel

TRINIDAD

62°W

61°W

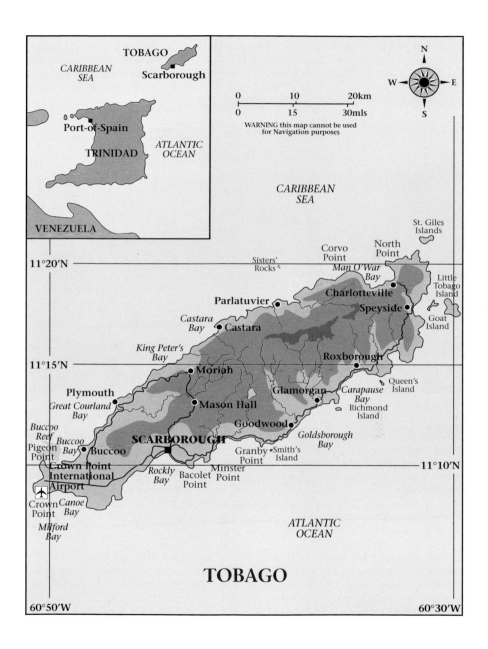

TOBAGO

CARIBBEAN
SEA

Scarborough

Port-of-Spain

TRINIDAD

ATLANTIC
OCEAN

VENEZUELA

N
W   E
S

0	10	20km
0	15	30mls

WARNING this map cannot be used
for Navigation purposes

CARIBBEAN
SEA

St. Giles
Islands

Corvo
Point

North
Point

11°20'N

Sisters'
Rocks

Man O'War
Bay

Little
Tobago
Island

Charlotteville

Parlatuvier

Speyside

Goat
Island

Castara
Bay

Castara

King Peter's
Bay

Roxborough

11°15'N

Moriah

Plymouth

Glamorgan

Carapause
Bay

Queen's
Island

Great Courland
Bay

Mason Hall

Richmond
Island

Buccoo
Reef

Goodwood

Buccoo
Bay

Goldsborough
Bay

Pigeon
Point

Buccoo

SCARBOROUGH

Granby
Point

Smith's
Island

Crown Point
International
Airport

Rockly
Bay

Bacolet
Point

Minster
Point

11°10'N

Crown
Point

Canoe
Bay

Milford
Bay

ATLANTIC
OCEAN

TOBAGO

60°50'W

60°30'W

Geography

The islands differ from the rest of the Caribbean Antilles in that they were once part of South America and attached to Venezuela. Massive flooding by the Orinoco, thousands of years ago, separated the islands from Venezuela. This is why the flora, fauna, and natural resources, especially petroleum, are similar to the Venezuelan mainland and there is more varied wildlife than the rest of the West Indies. The islands are believed to be continuations of the coastal Andes cordillera.

View of the city from Lady Young lookout

Trinidad is now separated from the South American continent by a channel of water called the Gulf of Paria. The Chaguaramas peninsula at the northwest of the island, extends with a series of small islands called the Bocas Islands and is separated at its closest point to Venezuela by the Dragon's Mouth. The main Bocas Islands are Chacachacare, Gasper Grande, Monos, Carrera and Huevos, covering an area of 1.75 sq miles (4.53 sq. km). There are also many other much smaller islets such as Five Islands and the Diego Islands. The southern peninsula of Trinidad extends to what is called the Serpent's Mouth in the Gulf of Paria.

From the closest point Tobago is 21 miles (33km) away from Trinidad, separated by the Columbus Passage. Tobago is volcanic in origin, but has no volcanoes and only one main mountain ridge. The western tip of the island is very low and flat but the topography changes from the central area to the eastern tip, as the land rises to a peak of 1860 ft (567 m).

History

The islands of Trinidad and Tobago were first discovered by Christopher Columbus on his third voyage in 1498. He named Trinidad (Spanish for Trinity) when he first saw the three hills in the southern part of the island. The islands were already inhabited by the Native American tribes, Arawaks and Caribs, collectively known as the

Amerindians. The Arawaks were the more peaceful tribe while the Caribs were hostile warriors who allegedly practised cannibalism. After Columbus' claim for Spain, the majority of Amerindians were annihilated. At present there are no surviving Arawaks and negligible Carib heritage in the country. However, the Amerindian presence is still found in the names of towns such as Arima, Piarco, Guayaguayare, Naparima, Mucurapo, Tunapuna, Chacachacare, Chaguaramas and Caroni, among a few others.

Parliament is convened at the historic Red House in Port of Spain

The British took rule in 1797, after a turbulent past of invasions by the Dutch and French. Trinidad became a British colony in 1802, while Tobago was ceded to Britain in 1814 by the French. Trinidad and Tobago became a single colony on April 6, 1889. The Spanish and French influence can again be seen in names of towns: Valencia, San Juan, Santa Cruz and Sans Souci, L'Anse Fourmi, Pointe-à-Pierre and Matelot, respectively. During the various invasions and reigns, much of the land was transformed into plantations with cocoa, sugar cane, coffee, coconuts and cotton. The slave trade supplied the labour needed for these agricultural enterprises. Slaves came in their droves from the west-central coast of Africa until slavery was abolished in 1834.

Apprenticeship followed for four years after that until emancipation became official on August 1, 1838. Most of the freed slaves left the sugar plantations creating a gap in the labour supply. The colonialists then decided to import workers from India and the system of indentureship was created. The first group of indentured labourers arrived in Trinidad on the *Fatel Rozack* on May 30, 1845. When indentureship ended in 1917, the Indians were offered free passage back home or a parcel of land to live on in Trinidad. Those who stayed brought their religion, cuisine and culture with them, which further enriched the fabric of Trinidadian society.

In the mid-19th century Portuguese immigrants from Madeira, off the Moroccan coast, began to arrive. They opted more for business instead of plantation work and farming like the Indians as they could not speak English and the work affected their health. There was also a small influx of Chinese indentured labourers between 1853 and 1866

Oil refinery at Pointe-à-Pierre

but the majority of Chinese immigrants came to Trinidad after 1911 and the numbers increased until the 1940s. The Syrian–Lebanese presence began around 1902 and today, although a very small community, dominates trade and distribution business in Trinidad.

Trinidad and Tobago gained independence from Britain in 1962 and joined the British Commonwealth. Dr Eric Williams was inaugurated as the first Prime Minister. The country then became a Republic in 1976 with its own President. The 1970s was the decade of an oil boom but the 1980s brought a recession which forced the Trinidad & Tobago dollar to be devalued and floated against the US dollar. The state-owned sugar industry also continued on a steady decline.

By the 1990s, there was a new surge in natural gas production and demand. Methanol and ammonia plants were also set up in the southern area of Trinidad. Unfortunately, as the economy continued to rely on the petrochemical sector for the majority of economic growth, a once thriving agriculture sector dwindled and now only contributes less than 2% of GDP. Tobago was targeted for development as a Tourism destination and has since offered tourists a pristine, non-commercialised choice of beaches and an array of watersports.

Population and Culture

The total population of Trinidad & Tobago is 1,262,366 million (2000). Tobago alone has a much smaller population of 54,084 (2000). There are two major ethnic groups, those of African and Indian descent. Together they account for just over 80% of the population in almost equal proportions, with the balance being smaller populations of mixed heritage, Chinese, Middle Eastern and European descent. The local Indians are referred to as 'East Indian' to distinguish from 'West Indian' ancestry and to avoid ambiguity with 'Native American Indian'. The majority of Indians live in Trinidad given their history with the sugar cane plantations in colonial times and most have preserved their strong religious and cultural heritage in the form of various Hindu and Muslim observances as well as in their cuisine, music and dance. Certain schools also teach Hindi and Arabic in conjunction with the respective religion.

Downtown at Independence Square, Port of Spain

The term 'Creole' refers to both foreign ancestry as well as those born locally. Creoles were identified in the 19th century with two groups: the French and African settlers. Hence, 'Creole cuisine' has endowed Trinidad & Tobago with many sumptuous dishes, characteristic of the country. A smaller community with a Spanish-Creole heritage is responsible for the indigenous Parang music, which is heard during the Christmas season. The villages of Paramin and Lopinot are the centres of live Parang performances and competitions from September to January.

The 85 foot Karyasidhdhi Hanuman Murti at Carapichaima was constructed in May 2003

The religious composition consists of approximately 29.4% Roman Catholic, 23.8% Hindu, 10.9% Anglican, 7.5% Pentecostal, 5.8% Muslim, 3.7% Seven Day Adventist, 3.4% Presbyterian and the balance in other beliefs including, Baha'i, Orisha (Shango), the Shouter Baptist Faith and non-religious or unknown.

Religious observances of the Hindus include, Divali or Deepavali (The Festival of Lights), Holi or Phagwa and Ramleela. The Muslim festivals include Eid ul Fitr and Hosay. Only Eid ul Fitr and Divali are considered public holidays.

Christian public holidays are granted for Corpus Christi, Good Friday, Easter Monday, Christmas Day and Boxing Day.

The most renowned cultural festival is Carnival which takes place on the Monday and Tuesday preceding Ash Wednesday. It is believed that Trinidadian Carnival, while synonymous with New Orleans Mardi Gras, originated with the enslaved Africans on the sugar plantations. The majority of customs and characters are clearly African. Nowadays, Carnival has grown from traditional masquerading to massive bands that burst with colour and creativity in the form of visually appealing costumes. A main theme is often used for each band and then various masqueraders assemble into each particular section of that band. The Band of the Year is a coveted title for bandleaders and participants.

Women clad in saris *lighting* deyas *on Divali evening*

Carnival costume on parade

The Carnival season is also the time of year when the national instrument, the steelpan, is most seen and heard. Panorama is a major competition where steelbands, with hundreds of steelpan players, vie for the prestigious first place. Calypso Monarch finals and the King and Queen of Carnival competition also take place on Dimanche Gras (Fat Sunday), just before the official parade of bands begins on Carnival Monday and Tuesday.

The steelpan is considered the national instrument of Trinidad & Tobago

Yachting facilities are convenient along the northwest peninsula of Trinidad

Airline Connections

Trinidad is served by major airlines such as American Airlines, American Eagle (via Puerto Rico), Air Canada, Continental, Air France (via Martinque and French Guiana), Caribbean Star, LIAT, Aeropostal, Rutaca, Avior, Surinam Airways and the national airline, BWIA. There are also several miscellaneous charter flights to North America such as Trans Meridian, World Airways, Air Transat and Sky Service. The Piarco International airport code is POS.

BWIA, the official airline of Trinidad & Tobago

Tobago also offers direct links to the United Kingdom via British Airways, Virgin Atlantic and the charters, JMC and Excel. Other European carriers include Condor, Air Lauda and Martinair. Tobago Express provides a daily air bridge service between Trinidad and Tobago on Dash 8 aircraft. The flight takes about 20 minutes and costs TT$200 (about US$34) return. The Crown Point International airport code is TAB.

Domestic Commuting

Car rental is the most convenient option for the actively mobile vacationer. Prices usually average about US$40 per day for an air-conditioned sedan, but could vary depending on the make, engine size and duration of rental. Since Trinidad & Tobago is a former British colony, driving has remained on the left side of the road.

For the visitor on an exclusive dive holiday, most dive shops can arrange pick-ups and drop-offs depending on the location of the hotel. In Tobago, the main dive areas are within easy access from

Maxi taxis are a popular mode of domestic commuting

most guesthouses and hotels so it is easy to coordinate with the dive centres before scheduled diving days.

Regular and privately hired taxis are frequently available. There is no metering system and prices are either fixed or negotiable. It is also common to see Maxi Taxis, which are mini buses that use a colour code to indicate which route the taxi serves. The public bus service is the cheapest form of mass movement available. All hired transport vehicles are identified by an 'H' as the first letter on the registration plates.

An inter-island ferry service is offered by the Port Authority for those who want the cheaper alternative to airline travel or for carrying automobiles and cargo between both islands. The trip is about 5 hours long and the *MF Panorama* and *MV Beauport* operate from the dock in Port of Spain to Scarborough and back. A new ferry service using the *MV Sonia* commenced in December 2004. Seasonal leases of fast ferries, *The Lynx* and *The Cat* now enable inter-island travel in less than three hours.

One of the inter-island ferries, MF Panorama

Climate

The two seasons are the dry and wet seasons. The dry season is from January to May and the wet season is from June to December. The average water temperature is 26°C in Tobago, but Trinidad tends to have more variable and lower temperatures, very often with thermoclines. Daytime temperature can soar regularly to as high as 34°C in the dry season with night-time lows of about 24°C. The average humidity is 75% in the dry season and 81% in the wet season. The cooler, wetter months average 32°C in the daytime with night temperatures of 22°C.

The Atlantic hurricane season lasts from July to December with most of the activity occurring from September to November. However, Trinidad and Tobago are so far south in the Caribbean that the islands are on the periphery of the hurricane belt and no major threats have been posed for many years, until recently with Hurricane Ivan in September 2004.

Windsurfing is very popular in Tobago

Maracas beach is Trinidad's favourite beach

Clothing

Cotton is the best choice of clothing material for the high daytime temperatures, high UV (ultraviolet) exposure and humidity. Trousers, jeans, shorts, jerseys, shirts or dresses are all acceptable forms of clothing. Comfortable shoes, sport sandals or flip-flops can be alternated depending on the type of walking or visit that is planned.

On the dive boat, it is essential to bring a hat or cap, as most of the boats do not have covered tops. A sunblock lotion with a high SPF rating is advisable to protect from severe and painful skin blistering. Towels and a change of clothing along with drinking water should be included in a personal bag.

Health Advisory

Trinidad & Tobago has a wide variety of medicines from all the leading pharmaceutical companies, such as Merck, GlaxoSmithKline, Aventis, Pfizer, Eli Lilly and others. It is thus quite easy to fill prescriptions and purchase essential OTC (over the counter) drugs during your vacation. Many cheaper generic forms or non-brand-name pharmaceuticals are common alternatives, as there are very good imports from India and other Caribbean countries or from a few local manufacturers.

If use of the public health service is not desired or is inconvenient, there are numerous private doctors, hospitals and clinics available at a higher cost.

There are no endemic forms of disease. Blood-sucking insects are a fact in the tropics and can leave very itchy, unattractive red blotches on the skin if one is not properly prepared. It is best to use effective insect repellents containing at least 25% DEET (diethyltoluamide), or new alternatives such as Picaridin or Oil of Lemon Eucalyptus.

Water is very safe for drinking but there is an abundant supply of imported and local brands of bottled water available at most resorts, groceries and supermarkets, for those who want to be vigilant.

Food-borne illnesses are also minimal but this is more linked to a personal choice of where to eat as related to safety and hygiene in food preparation. It is your right to inquire about ingredients used and when the meal was actually prepared, before purchasing. Beware of raw shellfish and undercooked meats to avoid the risk of gastroenteric infections.

At the time of writing, there has not been any case of SARS (Severe Acute Respiratory Syndrome) but a preparedness programme was implemented by the Ministry of Health and CAREC (Caribbean Epidemiology Center).

Unfortunately, Trinidad & Tobago has one of the highest prevalences of HIV/AIDS per capita in the Caribbean. It is a personal choice whether to take precautions or simply abstain from the risk of this and other sexually transmitted diseases.

Entry Requirements

No visa is required for citizens of the United States, European Union and British Commonwealth, with the exception of Australia, New Zealand, Sri Lanka, Nigeria, Papua New Guinea, Tanzania, Uganda, South Africa and India. A passport must be valid for 3 months longer than the intended stay or at least 6 months for some countries.

Cruise ship docked at Scarborough, Tobago

Money

The national currency is the Trinidad & Tobago dollar or $TT. At present, it floats against the $US and the rate of exchange has been stable over the past few years, at TT$6.30 to US$1 selling and TT$6 to US$1 buying cash. The dollar denominations are colour coded in notes of $1 (red), $5 (green), $10 (grey), $20 (purple) and $100 (blue).

$US cash is readily acceptable as are travellers' cheques or credit cards. Foreign currency can be converted at the bureau de change in the airports, money transfer agencies or at various banks. The main banks are Scotiabank, Royal Bank, First Citizens Bank, Republic Bank and Inter Commercial Bank.

Taxes

The major indirect tax is 15% VAT (Value Added Tax) on goods and services.

Hotels and restaurants also charge a 10% service tax. Tipping is optional unless already covered as part of the bill. Many satisfied divers have the option to leave personal or crew tips for divemasters, instructors and shop personnel.

The international Departure Tax is a standard TT$100 when leaving Trinidad & Tobago.

The financial towers in downtown Port of Spain

Telecommunications

The state owned TSTT (Telecommunications Services of Trinidad & Tobago) is currently the sole provider of telecommunications services. There are many landlines and mobile phone signal sites throughout both islands and the new GSM network allows international roaming and global connectivity. It is best to check the company's website www.tstt.net for more information on new services and mobile phone compatibility if planning to use one from another country during your visit.

Phone booths are at convenient locations and some utilise coins but many require phone cards, which can be purchased at various business outlets, hotels or at the airports.

Cyber cafés are now commonplace and mostly available throughout the busy areas of both islands. Rates vary from TT$15 to TT$25 per half-hour depending on the location.

Hotels, guesthouses and many homes have paid access to many premium cable TV channels and Direct TV™ with a Latin American feed.

Carnival masqueraders parade through the streets of Port of Spain

Photography

There are many stores offering one-hour photo processing and printing. For divers who plan to do a PADI scuba diving course, photos can be done locally or to save time, simply bring a few personal passport-sized photos from home.

Slide or E6 processing is only available in Trinidad.

Digital photography is still new to many locals and the range of cameras and accessories is very limited and very expensive. It is best to bring extra storage media, batteries or accessories specific to the land or underwater photography system being used. Dive centers do not yet offer professional photography or videography services but customers are welcome to bring their own equipment on dives at anytime. Video format is NTSC.

Electricity

Electrical current is both 110 and 220 volts at 60 cycles.

Highlands Waterfall, Highlands, Tobago

Time Zone

Trinidad & Tobago is –4 hours GMT (Greenwich Mean Time) and +1 hour EST (Eastern Standard Time). Daylight savings time is not utilised.

Satellite-derived positions

Positions obtained from satellite navigation systems, such as the Global Positioning System (GPS), are normally referenced to the World Geodetic System 1984 Datum. Such positions must be adjusted by 0.22 minutes SOUTHWARD and 0.05 minutes WESTWARD before plotting them on an Admiralty chart. For example:

Satellite-Derived Position (WGS 84 Datum)	11°09.50N	060°43.80W
Latitude/Longitude adjustment	0.22S	0.05W
Adjusted position	11°09.28N	060°43.85W

Also note that most navigational charts will indicate the GPS Datum used, whether it's the WGS 84 or another datum.

The GPS coordinates in this book were obtained with a Garmin 76 GPS using the WGS 84 Datum.

Yachting Services and Marinas

Tobago has no facilities for yacht maintenance and no marinas. In contrast, Trinidad has developed a flourishing and vibrant yachting and boat-building/repair industry and there are many reliable marinas. These are concentrated along the Chaguaramas peninsula where there are two dry docks and many businesses and chandleries dealing with boating and fishing tackle supplies. The website of the Yacht Services Association Trinidad & Tobago provides more contact information at www.ysatt.org

Yachts moored at one of the marinas in Chaguaramas

Cuisine

Indigenous dishes are among the most palatable and highly seasoned in the Caribbean. The multi-ethnic melange of people has resulted in a diverse choice of food and fusion cookery. Creole cuisine is a combination of African and Caribbean creativity that has characteristic dishes such as pelau, calalloo, buljol, oil down, coo coo. (See ethnic food glossary, page 102.)

A doubles vendor

Some areas of Trinidad and Tobago are associated with particular dishes: Curry crab and dumpling with Tobago; Shark and bake with Maracas Bay, Trinidad; Doubles with Debe, Piarco, El Socorro and Curepe all in Trinidad.

The East Indian presence has also created a distinct Caribbean type of food. Indian food in Trinidad is quite different from that of the Indian sub-continent. The curry blends are stronger and spicier. Roti is a common form of Indian flatbread made in three main types locally. Doubles, an Indo-Trinidadian creation, is the cheapest, most immediate and filling meal and is versatile as breakfast, lunch or dinner. Chinese, European and Middle Eastern restaurants are more common in Trinidad and especially along Ariapita Avenue in Port of Spain. American fast food franchises such as KFC, Tony Roma's, Pizza Hut, Subway, TGI Friday's, Papa John's and Church's are present.

Market vendors display their produce

A word of caution: Trinidadians and Tobagonians associate 'pepper' with the mouth-scorching Congo peppers of the *Capsicum* sp. not black or white pepper of the milder *Piper* sp. When asking for this spice, it would be presented in the form of a very pungent hot sauce. Be specific in distinguishing what type of pepper is required as hot peppers and condiments with them will cause severe and adverse reactions to those who are not familiar with their potency.

Topside Attractions

Trinidad offers more ecotourism and diverse activities than Tobago. However, the beaches are located far from the capital and are not as calm and beautiful as those in the sister isle. The more popular ones are Maracas Bay, Las Cuevas, Macqueripe, Manzanilla and Toco.

Peacock roaming freely at the Pointe-à-Pierre Wild Fowl Trust

Ecotourists and avid bird watchers frequent protected areas such as the Asa Wright Nature Center & Lodge and the Pointe à Pierre Wildfowl Trust. Other nature lovers can join groups on hikes or field trips to the more remote areas of the country where they can see the mud volcanoes of Hindustan, the Pitch Lake in La Brea, the Caroni Swamp and Bird sanctuary, the Bush-Bush Nature reserve in Nariva, hike to the summit of El Tucuche (the second highest mountain) or even visit the caves of Aripo or Cumaca where oilbirds reside. The nesting season for leatherback turtles is from March to August and visitors with permits are allowed to visit beaches such as Matura, Rincon or Grand Riviere.

A 'down the islands' expedition by boat to the Bocas Islands, offers visits to Gasparee Caves at Gaspar Grande or Salt Pond on Chacachacare with its enormous green iguanas. Chacachacare also has the dilapidated remnants of the Leprosarium, which was constructed in 1922 to 1926 and administered by the French Dominican nuns for decades. The Hansenian Settlement, which was practically a small city with its own generator, cinema, bakery and chapel amongst other amenities, finally stopped operations in 1984 and the last patients

KIRWIN SAMPSON/KEISHA SANDY

Young anglers displaying their prized dolphinfish at the International Game Fishing Tournament

left. Further exploration around Chacachacare, from Perruquier Bay, entices adventure seekers to a strenuous uphill walk to one of the tallest lighthouses in the world at the island's highest point of 2687 ft (818 m), with a perfect view of nearby Venezuela.

Water activities around the Trinidad mainland take place along the Chaguaramas peninsula where fishing, kayaking, yachting and sailing are widespread. There is also the annual power boat race, the Great Race, from Trinidad to Tobago, held every July.

Some of the finer beaches in Tobago include, Pigeon Point, Store Bay, Englishman's Bay, Parlatuvier and Mt Irvine. A rainforest tour to the Tobago Forest Reserve is a worthwhile trip as are those to other bird sanctuaries such as Little Tobago and St Giles islets.

The annual Goat and Crab Race takes place on Easter weekend while the Tobago Heritage Festival is from July to August and entertains many with folk music, dance and skits. The International Game Fishing Tournament is towards the end of April and the Angostura International Regatta is in May. Those who want to see the Buccoo Reef and visit the Nylon Pool can take tours in glass-bottom boats or snorkel close to shore.

Parlatuvier Bay

Diving Specifics

Type of tanks

Tanks are aluminium, yolk type K-valve and are available in 80 cu ft (10 litre) sizes. It is recommended that divers with DIN regulators bring an adaptor since most dive centres may not stock them.

Type of air

All centres provide regular compressed air. Nitrox is available at only two dive centres: World of Watersports and Undersea Tobago (see page 104).

Type of boat and layout

Almost all the dive boats are pirogue-style and most are open top. There is limited space for personal items and large dive bags should be left at the dive centre or hotel. A back roll is the choice of entry and exit is via a ladder hung over the side of the boat.

Type of dives

All dives on the Atlantic side of the island are done as a drift. Current is non-existent on the Caribbean side.

Certifications

All dive centres offer PADI courses and accept divers certified by other agencies. A certification card and log book must therefore be presented to the dive centre as proof of experience.

Typical boat entry from shore

Technician monitoring gauges on the hyperbaric chamber

Hyperbaric Chamber

There is a recompression facility (hyperbaric chamber) in Roxborough, Tobago. It was started in 2000 and was designed as a mono-place (one tender, one patient) chamber. For emergencies call Mr Kirwin Sampson at 789-9682 or Pager: 625-5472 #28843. All reputable dive centres should have specific protocol for dealing with dive accidents.

Bathers at Store Bay, one of the more popular beaches in Tobago

Yellowhead jawfish

DIVING IN TRINIDAD

Trinidad can only offer limited and seasonal diving because of discharge from the nearby Orinoco River in Venezuela. This causes high turbidity and very poor visibility for diving. When there is good visibility it is very transient and ranges from a depth of 16 to 100 ft (5 m to 30 m). During the rainy season from June to December, the turbidity is at its highest as the silt-laden influx of fresh water from the Orinoco flushes into the Gulf of Paria and along the north coast of Trinidad. The discharge from local rivers such as the Caroni contributes to characteristic turbid conditions. During the dry season, good visibility is still unpredictable and transient. The most distinguishing feature of Trinidad's water is its dark green colour. There are also occasional 'red tides' or HAB's (Harmful Algal Blooms). Do not expect the vibrant shades of blue often associated with the other waters of the Caribbean islands and even Tobago.

The seasonal variations in salinity and turbidity hinder proper coral reef development in Trinidad. Symbiosis between hard corals and zooxanthellae require very consistent and precise conditions if reef formation is to occur. The diving is therefore limited to only certain areas along the north coast and around the Bocas Islands. The waters around Trinidad are rich in plankton and sightings of large mantas are quite common as this is their main source of food. Unlike Tobago, encounters with large pelagic fish are almost guaranteed as are thermoclines that occur at varying depths but can usually be found at around 33 ft (10 m). Water temperature can drop as low as 16°C. Diving in Trinidad is more of an adventure than the pretty, colour bursts of reef life offered in Tobago.

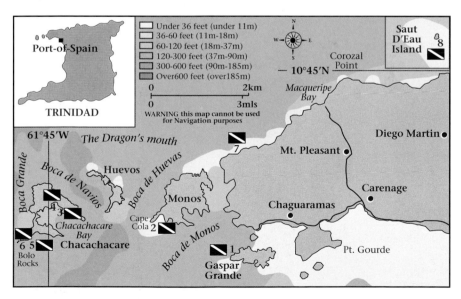

1 POINT BALEINE

DEPTH RANGE: 20–100 ft (6–30 m)
DIVING EXPERIENCE: Beginner
GPS: N10°39.849 / W061°39.985

Once a whaling station, Point Baleine is regarded as an excellent fishing and diving area because of the prolific fish life that can be found here. The reef slopes acutely to the bottom and gives the appearance of a wall dive. The extensive, unexplored cavern system along the reef hides enormous Goliath groupers and snappers. Large spiny lobsters and variegated sea urchins can be found in the many cracks and crevices formed from the numerous boulders that cover the reef. Look for banded coral shrimps and yellowline arrow crabs in overhangs.

White telesto is one type of octocoral

Pelagic jacks, Atlantic spadefish and rainbow runners can often be seen in the open water. French grunts and yellowtail snappers, grey and French angelfish abound.

Avoid touching the reef since most of the rocks are inhabited and covered by large colonies of feather hydroids and stinging bush hydroids. Fire corals, regal sea fans, wide-mesh sea fans and carmine sea sprays exist but in limited numbers. Flower corals and solitary disk corals speckle the reef. At the deeper end look for numerous devil's sea whips and wire corals.

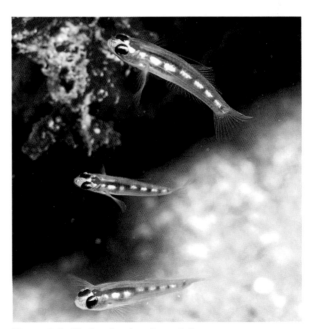

Tiny masked gobies hovering above the sea bed

2 POINT COURANT

DEPTH RANGE: 17-90 ft (5–27 m)
DIVING EXPERIENCE: Intermediate
GPS: N10°40.950 / W061°42.046

Located at the southeastern end of Monos Island, Point Courant (French for 'current') is a fast, exhilarating dive that rewards the diver with a wide variety of marine life. The strong current keeps silt off the reef and continuously feeds the coral with plankton-rich water, hence they look much healthier than in other areas. Starting at 17 ft (5 m) of water in a calm bay, with very little coral and fish life, the dive heads south. Meandering around enormous silt covered boulders, the dive then continues east and drops off to around 66 ft (20 m). Here the reef comes alive with shoals of grunts, snappers, damselfish, groupers and thousands of bait fish. Caribbean spiny lobsters can be found in large numbers under rocks and overhangs. Juvenile yellowtail damselfish, (commonly referred to as jewelfish) harlequin bass, parrotfish and butterflyfish abound. Yellowprow gobies can be found diligently at work at the dozens of cleaning stations. The reef is covered with a mix of hard and soft corals and an array of sponges.

Upon approach to the south-eastern tip of the island, the current increases and moves in a westerly direction going into deeper water. Navigating with the land on the right and swimming a short distance against the current brings you around the tip of the reef into a calm bay. The current is non-existent and the dive continues in a northerly direction. Here the reef drops off sharply, almost vertically, to a sandy sea bed and the marine life here is much the same. It is quite normal to encounter giant mantas feeding on the plankton-rich water. Large hawksbill turtles are often sighted foraging on sponges.

Caribbean reef squid during a night dive at Point Courant

3 DOCTOR'S REEF

DEPTH RANGE: 10–70 ft (3–21 m)
DIVING EXPERIENCE: Beginner
GPS: N10°41.039 / W061°44.243

Starting in a calm, shallow bay, the dive heads west along the boulder-covered reef that has a steep gradient to a sandy bottom then heads in a north-westerly direction. The corals here are mainly rigid red telesto, feather hydroids and small sea fans. Green solitary disk corals can be found at the shallower end. While the coral growth may not be impressive, the fish life certainly is. Enormous groupers, snappers and hogfish are regularly seen roaming the reef. Queen angelfish, parrotfish and triggerfish congregate in large numbers. You will pass through several layers of thermoclines on this dive and the temperature change can be dramatic.

A dive light is recommended as you are likely to find green moray eels and spiny lobsters hiding in the rocks' holes and crevices. Look for large hawksbill turtles under overhangs. Spotted scorpionfish lie camouflaged close to the rocks. The dive ends in the shallow sandy beach-front of Rust's Bay. A magnificent house that was once the living quarters of the leprosarium's doctor, is located in the bay, hence the name of the reef.

A separate dive can be executed from shore in this bay where some of the largest flying gurnards can be found. On the sandy sea bed look for yellowhead jawfish, banded jawfish and bridled gobies. There are many colonies of corkscrew anemones with their companion Pedersen cleaning shrimps and red snapping shrimps. Peppermint cleaning shrimps flourish in large numbers and can often be seen in cracks and crevices.

A peppermint shrimp waiting at its cleaning station

4 THE KITCHEN

DEPTH RANGE: 20–70 ft (6–21 m)
DIVING EXPERIENCE: Beginner
GPS: N10°40.535 / W061°43.593

This reef gets its name from the leprosarium that was operational on the island from 1926 to 1984. Left-over food and table scraps from the kitchen were dumped over the cliff onto the reef below. Not only was food dumped but bottles, various crockery and any other useless utensils. These can still be found on the dive. Despite being a previous dumping ground, the sloping reef has flourished and is composed of large boulders covered with small wide-mesh sea fans, carmine sea sprays, finger corals and feather brush hydroids. At the base of the rocks look for magnificent feather dusters and brown fan worms. Rough fileclams can be found in large quantities in narrow cracks and crevices displaying their brilliant red to orange-red mantle. The yellowline arrow crabs here are unusually large and can be found together with a variety of other crustaceans.

Sergeant majors, butterflyfish, fairy basslets, queen angelfish and other varieties of fish add colour to this dull grey, silt-covered reef. Yellowhead Jawfish, bridled gobies and lizard fish can be found on the sandy sea bed. Look under overhangs and in the large cracks between boulders for giant hawksbill turtles. Spanish or 'shovel-nosed' lobsters are common but are difficult to recognise since they are well camouflaged against the rocks.

File clams

5 DOKTOR SIEGERT

DEPTH RANGE: 24–27 ft (7–8 m)
DIVING EXPERIENCE: Beginner
GPS: N10°40.247 / W061°45.719

Originally named the *Otaki*, then *Doktor Siegert*, after Angostura's founder, Dr J.B.G. Siegert, this 204 ft (61.9 m) long wooden sailing ship regularly plied the trade between Trinidad and Venezuela often carrying cargoes of asphalt, Angostura aromatic bitters, coconuts and other miscellaneous items. On July 2, 1895 it set sail for Venezuela but had to anchor at La Tinta Bay on the western side because of a flat calm. Conditions were not favourable on this side and the captain decided to go into a sheltered bay on the southern end. Strong under-currents caused the ship to drift onto the nearby Bolo rocks and it was severely damaged. It started to leak and eventually sank on July 4 and now lies at 25 ft (7.8 m) on a sandy sea bed. Over the past century numerous storms have battered and broken the ship, leaving the timbers dispersed over a wide area.

The *Doktor Siegert* is now home to diverse species of marine life. Goliath groupers (jewfish), large spiny lobsters and metre-long green morays can be found in the upturned hull or in the large crevices formed by the timbers. Enormous hawksbill turtles are often seen lying idly on the wreck and can be easily approached. Shoals of French and bluestriped grunts hover over the wreck swaying with the surge. Queen, grey and French angelfish also reside here together with several species of butterflyfish. Look for spotted eagle rays in groups of three or four 'flying' over the wreck. The timbers are heavily encrusted with large blue mussels and a carpet of algae.

The ship's anchor is located 130 ft (40 m) east of the wreck in about 28 ft (8.5 m) of water and is easily recognisable since it is sparsely covered with coral and is approximately 8 ft (2.5 m) long and 5 ft (1.5 m) wide.

A variegated feather duster worm with its calcareous tube in view

6 GERRY'S POINT

DEPTH RANGE: 20–66 ft (6–20 m)
DIVING EXPERIENCE: Advanced
GPS: N10°40.278 / W061°45.999

Named after one of the best divers in Trinidad who discovered it, Gerry's Point is a diver's dream. Located at the south-eastern tip of Chacachacare Island close to Bolo Rocks, the dive begins in 17 ft (5 m) and gradually descends to 33 ft (10 m). The current can be quite strong upon approach to the open channel. Because of the strong currents, the large boulders that comprise this reef are kept clean of silt and the corals are constantly fed with plankton-rich water.

Covered with wide-mesh sea fans, bent sea rods, flower corals, yellow tube sponges and sea fan hydroids, the rocks rise from a sandy bottom close to the surface. The numerous large, pelagic fish are the highlight of the dive. Large numbers of mantas swim in mid-water with their mouths agape filtering plankton. Small schools of scalloped hammerheads are observed on the sea bed, often feeding. Mutton snappers here can get up to 3 ft (1 m) in length and can be seen hiding in overhangs. Hawksbill turtles are often seen lazily swimming over the rocky reef regularly stopping to feed. Parrotfish, angelfish, butterflyfish, damselfish, scorpionfish, hogfish, jewfish, and queen triggerfish are just a sample of fish life on this dive.

Because of the constant flow of water, this is one of the few dives where the visibility is good enough for photographing the diverse marine life.

Yellowline arrow crab feeding on warty sea rod

7 MIRAGE

DEPTH RANGE: 24–100 ft (7–30 m)
DIVING EXPERIENCE: Advanced
GPS: N10°42.840 / W061°39.806

Located on Trinidad's north coast, Mirage is a bright, colourful, lively reef littered with marine life and is a favourite with experienced divers. Covered with a carpet of carmine sea sprays, yellow and violet wide-mesh sea fans, feather bush hydroids and large sea fans, the reef is made up of massive boulders with large holes that provide excellent hiding spots for spiny lobsters, green moray eels, black margates and fairy basslets. Because of the strong current, silt hardly has a chance to settle, so the corals here are very healthy.

Commencing in a calm bay, the dive travels in a northerly direction following the gentle slope of the reef towards the sandy sea bed, then heads west. The current is mild at first, increasing in speed as the channel between Trinidad and Monos Island is approached. Large pelagic jacks swim from the deep, over the reef and back out. Encounters with mantas and dolphins are quite common. Fish life is plentiful and includes butterflyfish, queen angelfish, shoals of grunts and sergeant majors. There are urchins, crabs and many other invertebrates tucked into the reef's nooks and crannies. Expect a thermocline at around 60 ft (18 m) where the temperature can drop to about 20 °C.

Bermuda chub on Mirage

8 SAUT D'EAU ISLAND

DEPTH RANGE: 24–83 ft (7–25 m)
DIVING EXPERIENCE: Advanced
GPS: N10°46.164 / W061°30.986

Located on the north coast, just next to La Vache Bay, Saut D'Eau Island's only inhabitants are pelicans and other sea birds. This site can only be dived when conditions are good. Because the reef breaks the surface, rough sea conditions can generate a very strong underwater surge. Dropping off on the eastern side of the fringing reef south of the island there is a quick drop down to the bottom on a sandy sea bed. The massive boulders that form the main reef have almost vertical walls with large cracks resembling caverns and are covered with encrusting sponges, large sea fans and a variety of octocorals. Because the salinity levels are much higher (less fresh water) the corals and sponges are healthier and bigger than the sites around the Bocas Islands. Visibility is also better since very little of the muddy Orinoco flow reaches this far north.

There is an impressive amount of fish life on the reef including large snappers, groupers, angelfish, butterflyfish, damselfish, parrotfish and shoals of grunts. Pelagics include tuna, dolphinfish, crevalle jack, African pompano, king mackerel and Atlantic spadefish. Mantas are often sighted in small groups of three or four and approach divers with curiousity. Look for large tarpons and barracudas near the surface close to the vertical walls.

Colourful queen angelfish swimming among rope sponges

Pigeon Point Beach, Tobago

DIVING IN TOBAGO

The problem of silting from the Orinoco River does not affect Tobago as adversely as it does Trinidad, given the distance between the two islands. The visibility is much better than around Trinidad but there can be turbid conditions in the dry season as the water temperature rises and plankton proliferates. This is a positive as larger, pelagic fishes prey on plankton or smaller fish. The Guyana Current brings nutrient-rich water, constantly bathing the reefs, while the Atlantic Current brings clear, blue water. Generally, the conditions of Tobago's marine environment are more favourable to sustained coral reef development as salinity, turbidity and water temperature do not fluctuate as in Trinidad.

The main areas of diving are: Columbus Passage, North Coast, Man O'War Bay, St Giles Islands and Speyside.

All diving in the **Columbus Passage** area is done as a drift because of the strong Atlantic currents. The water is almost always clean and blue with a proliferation of marine life and healthy coral. Because of the strong currents, all divemasters carry a surface marker buoy (SMB) that the dive boat follows. It is imperative to use the line attached to the SMB when ascending since it is easy to be swept away from the dive site.

Fringing reefs make up most of the dive sites in the **North Coast** area starting from Store Bay at the south-western end to as far as Sisters Rocks at the north-eastern side. The most noticeable aspect of this region is the lack of current, which favours photographers and inexperienced divers. Most of the dive sites are close to land and can be accessed from shore or from a dive boat. There are numerous white, sandy beaches and reefs close to shore that are ideal for snorkelling. Large pelagics are the highlight of this region.

Man O'War Bay at the northern tip of Tobago is sheltered from the northeast trade winds providing dive sites that are free from currents and large waves. The fishing village of Charlotteville is located here. All the dive sites are just minutes from the dive centre and are excellent for beginners.

St Giles Islands dive sites are found around a group of rocks located 0.6 m (1 km) off the north-eastern tip of Tobago. Here the Atlantic Ocean collides with the Caribbean Sea bringing strong currents and plankton-rich water that attracts some of the largest pelagics in Tobago. Dive sites are accessed by a short boat ride from Charlotteville.

Located on the east coast of Tobago, **Speyside** is regarded as one of the best dive regions in the Caribbean. The reefs are in pristine condition and are home to literally thousands of fish and other marine life. All diving is done as a drift and most dives are located around Little Tobago and Goat Island and are minutes from the docks.

Columbus Passage Dive Sites

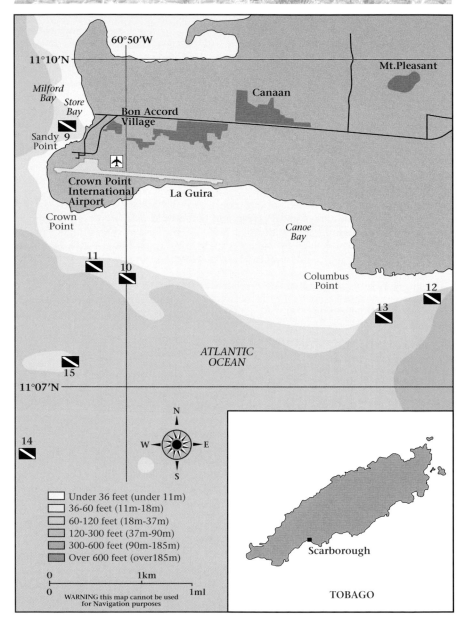

60°50'W

11°10'N

Mt.Pleasant

Milford Bay
Store Bay

Canaan

Bon Accord Village

Sandy Point
9

Crown Point International Airport

Crown Point

La Guira

Canoe Bay

Columbus Point

11

10

12

13

15

ATLANTIC OCEAN

11°07'N

N
W E
S

14

Under 36 feet (under 11m)
36-60 feet (11m-18m)
60-120 feet (18m-37m)
120-300 feet (37m-90m)
300-600 feet (90m-185m)
Over 600 feet (over185m)

0   1km
0   1ml
WARNING this map cannot be used
for Navigation purposes

Scarborough

TOBAGO

9 KARIWAK REEF

DEPTH RANGE: 10–55 ft (3–17 m)
DIVING EXPERIENCE: Beginner
GPS: N11°09.314 / W060°50.646

This reef is located about 130 ft (40 m) off Store Bay and is easily accessed directly from the shore or from a boat. The dive starts at a depth of 10 ft (3 m), proceeds in a westerly direction and can reach as deep as 52 ft (16 m). The reef slopes gently and ends on a flat, sandy sea bed. The absence of current in Kariwak Reef is an underwater photographer's delight offering an array of colour and marine life. Here the barrel sponges are perfectly shaped and not deformed as in other sites with heavy currents. Look inside for banded coral shrimps. A wide variety of hard and soft corals are found such as sea rods, sea plumes, sea whips, encrusting gorgonians, sea fans and fire corals. Large brain corals and mountainous star corals are often covered with Christmas tree worms and split-crown feather dusters.

Fish life includes Nassau groupers, balloon fish, lizardfish, shoals of blue and grey chromis and barracuda. Under overhangs look for large green moray eels and small spiny lobsters. Spotted eagle rays can often be seen gliding over the reef. Scorpionfish are abundant but often missed because they are well-camouflaged. Look for the sprightly damselfish, goatfish, parrotfish and shoals of grunt. On the sandy bottom you will find several flying gurnards 'walking' about on their finger-like spines of lower pectoral fins which are used like hands to turn over rubble when foraging. When alarmed, they spread their huge fan-like pectoral fins and swim away. Nudibranchs are common.

Banded coral shrimp are often found in pairs

10 FLYING REEF

DEPTH RANGE: 18–45 ft (6–14 m)
DIVING EXPERIENCE: Beginner
GPS: N11°08.102 / W060°49.976

This reef is located just about 2 miles (1.5 km) south of the Crown Point International Airport. The current on this dive varies from 1 knot to as much as 3 knots. Because of the length of this reef, the dive must be done as two separate dives referred to as lower (deeper) and upper (shallower) flying reef. The dive orients in a westerly direction and follows along the sandy edge of the gently sloping reef. Covered mainly by octocorals including sea rods, sea fans, sea plumes, sea sprays, star corals and a wide variety of sponges, the reef provides a healthy environment for the vast marine life that lives here.

Expect to find sleeping nurse sharks up to 7 ft (21 m) in length under overhangs, schools of blue and grey chromis, southern sennets and the ever-present giant green moray eels while hawksbill turtles can be seen foraging on the sponges. Stingrays are often concealed at the reef's edge under the sand and can go unnoticed. Spiny lobsters are abundant and found under rocks. Nassau groupers sit idly at the edge of the reef while many species of parrot fish, grunts and angelfish are also the highlights of this dive.

A hawksbill turtle resting

11 STINGRAY ALLEY

DEPTH RANGE: 30–50 ft (9–16 m)
DIVING EXPERIENCE: Beginner
GPS: N11°08.125 / W060°50.414

This dive starts at the end of Flying Reef and is much deeper. The current can be quite strong at times and the visibility varies from 26–39 ft (8–12 m). As the name suggests, numerous large southern stingrays are often seen gliding over the reef or buried just beneath the sand with their two large eyes peeering out. Also on the sandy sea bed look for lesser electric rays and Atlantic guitarfish.

Large boulders are covered with sea fans, knobby sea rods, slimy sea plumes and a variety of sponges form large holes where spiny lobsters and small green turtles or hawksbill turtles often hide. Look for pelagic jacks, schools of Atlantic spadefish and southern sennets in the deep. Queen angelfish, large midnight parrotfish and glasseye snappers are common.

Black tip reef sharks are often seen gliding over the top of the reef in search of food. There is also a good chance of seeing large nurse sharks beneath the numerous overhangs.

Southern stingrays are the highlight of Stingray Alley

12 COVE

DEPTH RANGE: 30–85 ft (9–26 m)
DIVING EXPERIENCE: Intermediate
GPS: N11°07.855 / W060°47.329

Located just south of Columbus Point, the Cove is actually an extension of Flying Reef. The current here can be very strong at times and generally travels in a westerly direction. The reef has a steep gradient and extends to a sandy sea bed and coral life includes Venus sea fans, fire corals, warty sea rods, encrusting gorgonians and brilliant sea fingers. There are patches of finger corals, mountainous star corals and large brain corals dotting the reef. Very long Devil's whips can be found at the deeper end of the reef.

At the edge of the reef look for large black groupers, cubera snappers and Caribbean spiny lobsters. On the sandy bottom look for stingrays, peacock flounders, yellowhead jawfish and small electric rays. Spotted and green moray eels can be seen hiding among the myriad of hard and soft corals. There are huge barrel sponges but most are bent out of shape owing to the strong current. The occasional small hawksbill turtles can be seen resting on the reef. Queen angelfish and several species of parrotfish abound.

Large green morays are common at Cove and make excellent photo subjects

13 COVE LEDGE

DEPTH RANGE: 18–48 ft (5–14 m)
DIVING EXPERIENCE: Beginner
GPS: N11°07.823 / W060°47.646

Also known as Cove Crack, the dive site gets its name from the numerous ledges and cracks in the reef. Since it is close to the rocky shoreline and is shallow, there is always a gentle surge at the beginning of the dive. However, when the seas are rough, the surge can be quite powerful. This drift dive initially starts off in a northerly direction then changes westward after dropping over the edge of the reef.

The reef is composed mainly of hard corals including brain coral, starlet coral, smooth star coral and fragile saucer coral. At the beginning of the dive there are massive elkhorn corals in pristine condition covering a wide area. This is probably the only known dive site where such large numbers of elkhorn corals are so prolific. Venus and common sea fans, angled perpendicular to the prevailing current, litter the sea floor, interspaced with small barrel sponges and yellow tube sponges.

There is a wide variety of fish life including queen and French angelfish, Bermuda chub, blue and brown chromis and parrotfish. A dive light is useful when peering under ledges for sleeping nurse sharks, hawksbill turtles, moray eels, groupers and a variety of snappers and grunts. Look for the ever present large barracudas hovering in mid-water, hiding beneath the overhangs or following divers around. Southern stingrays are also often sighted gliding over the reef or camouflaged beneath the sand.

A diver exploring one of the numerous overhangs

14 DIVER'S DREAM

DEPTH RANGE: 30–50 ft (9–15 m)
DIVING EXPERIENCE: Advanced
GPS: N11°06.600 / W060°51.327

This dive is located about 5 miles (8 km) southwest of Crown Point on Drew Shoal. Here the current is usually between 2 and 3 knots but can get to as much as 4 knots. Upon entering the water, descend directly to the bottom since it is possible to be carried away from the dive site by the surface current. Look for a plateau at 26 ft (8 m). Descend to 36 ft (11 m) and continue the dive. The visibility is usually between 50 and 260 ft (15 and 80 m). There are numerous hard corals of vivid colours. As you drift past between large boulders that rise almost to the surface look for bull sharks and blacktip reef sharks. Nurse sharks can be seen lying idly beneath enormous overhangs.

It is common to see eagle rays in pairs swimming past or hawksbill turtles resting on the sandy bottom. The barracudas here can grow up to 5 ft (1.5 m) long, are highly inquisitive and usually swim straight up to divers. The reef is littered with queen and French angelfish, parrotfish, green and spotted moray eels, hundreds of butterflyfish, large schools of grunts, bluehead wrasse and snappers. The giant barrel sponges are deformed by the strong currents and are bent over at an angle of 45° and they cover almost the entire dive site. The best time of year to dive this site is usually between March and June when there is little rainfall and visibility is unaffected by muddy land erosion and deposits.

A nurse shark on Diver's Dream

15 DIVER'S THIRST

DEPTH RANGE: 30–50 ft (9–15 m)
DIVING EXPERIENCE: Advanced
GPS: N11°07′204 / W060°50.509

Located a mile (1.8 km) north-east of Diver's Dream the reef is composed of a series of overlapping ledges. The coral is sparse, with deepwater sea fans, yellow tube sponges and hydroids on the side exposed to the current. The sheltered side consists of large misshaped barrel sponges, small octocorals, orange cup corals and large elkhorn corals. Beneath the ledges there are several large nurse sharks, turtles, spiny lobsters and green moray eels. Large blacktip reef sharks swim in small groups about the reef.

Angelfish, large midnight parrotfish, Creole wrasse, damselfish, snappers and several species of grouper are the dominant reef fish on this site.

The current is less strong here than at Diver's Dream. However, it can easily sweep you into deeper water. Monitor your computer or depth gauge constantly.

Clumps of yellow tube sponges

Large elkhorn coral

Yellow Tube Sponge

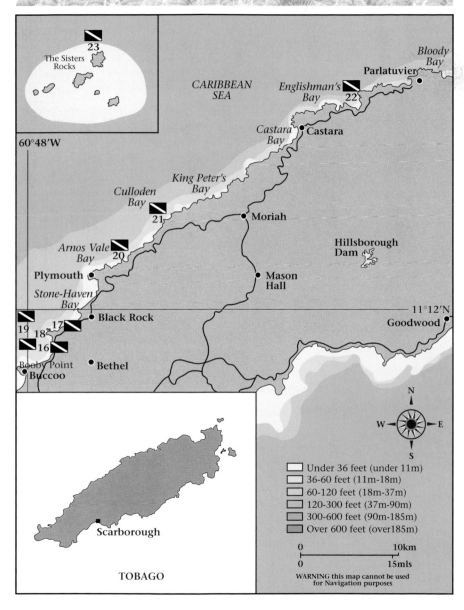

The Sisters Rocks 23

Bloody Bay

Parlatuvier

CARIBBEAN SEA

Englishman's Bay 22

Castara Bay Castara

60°48'W

King Peter's Bay

Culloden Bay 21

Moriah

Hillsborough Dam

Arnos Vale Bay 20

Plymouth

Stone-Haven Bay

Mason Hall

11°12'N

Black Rock

Goodwood

19 18 17

16

Booby Point   Bethel

Buccoo

N
W — E
S

Under 36 feet (under 11m)
36-60 feet (11m-18m)
60-120 feet (18m-37m)
120-300 feet (37m-90m)
300-600 feet (90m-185m)
Over 600 feet (over185m)

Scarborough

0   10km
0   15mls

WARNING this map cannot be used
for Navigation purposes

TOBAGO

16 DUTCHMAN'S REEF

DEPTH RANGE: 24–45 ft (7–14 m)
DIVING EXPERIENCE: Beginner
GPS: N11°11.669 / W060°47.906

This reef is easily accessed from either the shore at Mount Irvine beach or from a boat. The dive starts shallow and heads in a westerly direction. Along the reef's edge, look for two very old cannons that were once part of the Dutch East India Company fleet that ran aground in the 17th century. They can be difficult to recognise because of heavy coral encrustation. Once passed the cannons, the dive heads north and here the reef takes on a different appearance. The hard corals form huge holes that are home to spiny lobsters, the occasional nurse shark, blackbar soldierfish, cardinalfish and numerous arrowhead crabs. There are numerous cleaning stations along the reef consisting of corkscrew anemones with associated red snapping shrimps and tiny Pedersen cleaning shrimps. This part of the reef is covered by brown tube sponges, small brain corals, fire corals and black ball sponges. The mountainous star corals are heavily inhabited with Christmas tree worms and split-crown feather dusters. Black long-spined urchins dot the reef and contrast against the white hard corals.

On the second half of this dive, the reef slopes steeply to the sandy sea floor and here there is a profusion of soft corals consisting of sea rods, sea plumes, Venus sea fans, common sea fans, sea sprays and various sponges. The reef is home to a large shoal of Creole wrasse and blue and brown chromis. Large spiny lobsters and giant green moray eels are often found hiding under ledges at the reef's edge. On the sandy sea bed look for Southern stingrays, lesser electric rays, spotted snake eels and large yellowhead jawfish not to mention hawksbill turtles which normally feed on the smaller barrel sponges.

Carmouflaged scorpionfish have poisonous spines

17 MOUNT IRVINE WALL

DEPTH RANGE: 18–47 ft (6–14 m)
DIVING EXPERIENCE: Beginner
GPS: N11°12.003 / W060°47.823

Located just 3 minutes from Mount Irvine Beach facilities by boat, this wall dive has a maximum depth of 50 ft (15 m) and is actually a group of rocky outcroppings extending out to sea. The surge action can be quite strong at times and divers should avoid venturing near the top of the reef. The coral covering the wall is composed mainly of small yellow tube sponges, a fan-shaped greenish-grey variety of the branching vase sponge, black ball sponges, encrusting gorgonians, small black sea rods, porous sea rods, stinging bush hydroids and large quantities of social feather dusters. The Venus and common sea fans are often covered with finger-print cyphomas or flamingo tongues that prey on them. Look for miniscule tunicates attached to many of the soft corals.

There are many swim-through areas and crevices to explore. A dive light is recommended to shine into the cracks where shy cardinalfish, octopuses, juvenile spotted drums and many species of shrimps and crabs can be exposed.

There are dozens of cleaning stations along the reef where sharknose gobies and Pedersen cleaning shrimps tend to the wide variety of fish life. Large spotted snake eels bury themselves in the sandy sea bed with only their heads protruding, while sharptail eels meander through the many corals in search of food. There are vertical cracks and crevices along the wall where it is possible to see small hawksbill turtles, scorpionfish and shy blackbar soldier fish hiding. The highlight of this dive is at the end, where it is possible to see longsnout seahorses. Look for them at around 50 ft (15 m) wrapped around knobby sea rods. Though difficult to locate, they can easily be approached. However, when found, they will swim away if disturbed.

At night Mount Irvine Wall comes alive. Caribbean reef octopuses are out feeding on the many molluscs while giant basket stars that are usually hidden in the daytime extend their arms and form a fan-shaped plankton net. The myriad, resident long-spined urchins are seen feeding in the open.

A shy longsnout seahorse clinging to sea rods

18 MOUNT IRVINE EXTENSION

DEPTH RANGE: 23–72 ft (7–22 m)
DIVING EXPERIENCE: Beginner
GPS: N11°12.013 / W060°47.934

This dive is actually a continuation of the Mount Irvine Wall but the coral here is quite different, composed mainly of knobby sea rods, slit-pore sea rods, swollen-knob candelabrum, warty sea rods and small to medium sea fans. The many small brain corals are shrouded with Christmas tree worms and feather dusters. This reef is a spawning ground for many species of fish and the presence of millions of fry tends to give the water a milky appearance. Large black groupers and cubera snappers can often be seen in groups of three or four feeding on the fry.

Sharpnose pufferfish

The reef slopes steeply to a sandy sea bed where Southern stingrays, spiny lobsters, yellowhead jawfish and small snake eels can be seen. The deeper end of this reef is composed mainly of hard coral. Several small hawksbill turtles tend to forage on the soft coral and green algae at the shallower end of the reef. There are many queen, French and grey angelfish, almost all the species of parrot fish, large schools of blue and brown chromis, Creole fish and grunts. The numerous nooks and crannies conceal a variety of moray eels, fairy basslets, cardinalfish and banded coral shrimp.

A sharknose gobie at its cleaning station

19 MAVERICK WRECK

DEPTH RANGE: 53–100 ft (16–30 m)
DIVING EXPERIENCE: Advanced
GPS: N11°12.207 / W060°48.272

Previously a passenger, vehicle and cargo ferry that travelled between Trinidad and Tobago, the *Scarlet Ibis*, as it was originally named, went into service in 1959 and was retired in 1975. It was thoroughly cleaned of oil and other pollutants. Hatches and other entrapments were either removed or secured making all compartments of the ship completely accessible. On April 7, 1997 it was scuttled by the Association of Tobago Dive Operators and now sits upright on a sandy sea bed at a depth of 100 ft (30 m) with its bow pointing almost due north. Descending the permanent shot line attached to the stern, you pass through large shoals of sprats, anchovies and other baiting fish that provide food for the many bonito and false albacore tuna that swoop from the deep to feed. The main deck is at 75 ft (23 m) and just below that, at 90 ft (27.3 m), is the vehicle deck that runs the length of the ship where snappers and grunts assemble in large numbers. Visibility on the wreck is usually around 23–26 ft (7–8 m).

There are many open hatches on the vehicle deck where the engine room is easily accessed. Proper training and supervision is necessary before entry into this area of the ship. Exit from the vehicle deck is via a large hatch at the bow. The pilot house is at 56 ft (17 m) and entry is accessed from the many openings to the front. The highest point of the wreck is the smoke stack at 52 ft (16 m). The passenger cabins are located aft of the pilot house and below the smoke stack.

The highlight of this wreck is the resident great barracuda measuring approximately 7 ft (2 m) long and which can usually be found just above the smoke stack or within the pilot house. Indifferent to divers, they can easily be approached at close range. Beneath the stern, look for teardrop snappers and large spiny lobsters. Other residents include coney, moray eels, grunts, schools of Atlantic spadefish and southern sennet. Look for cleaning stations at the bow and stern where Pedersen cleaning shrimps and sharknose gobies are diligently at work. The hull and exposed decks are encrusted with red polyp octocorals, tunicates, sponges and literally thousands of Atlantic thorny oysters.

Cubera and yellowtail snappers on the bow of the wreck

20 ARNOS VALE

DEPTH RANGE: 16–45 ft (5–14 m)
DIVING EXPERIENCE: Beginner
GPS: N11°13.806 / W060°45.986

This reef is accessed by boat or off the beach at the Arnos Vale Hotel and is made up of several large boulders covered by a variety of hard and soft corals. It is almost flat except for along the wall and is excellent for both diving and snorkelling. The dive starts on the shallow, sandy sea bed and then heads in a north-easterly direction following the edge of the reef. The surge can be strong at times, depending on surface conditions, because most of the diving is done along the steep face of the rocks close to shore.

Octocorals cover a major part of the flat reef and include sea fans, sea rods, sea sprays and sea plumes. Stony corals include brain corals and star corals, finger corals, flower corals and to a small extent, elkhorn corals. Fish life includes angelfish, parrotfish, trunkfish, spotted drums, damselfish, butterflyfish, gobies, blennies, arrowhead crabs, banded coral shrimps and numerous sergeant majors. Look for the very small, benthic, green razorfish above the sandy bottom, near rocks or gorgonians. When alarmed, it curls its body as a form of mimicry akin to a leaf and often ducks into the sand for refuge.

Arnos Vale reef makes an excellent night dive with several large octopus, scorpionfish, batfish, moray eels and basketstar fish coming out to feed.

Juvenile spotted drum hides in cracks and crevices

Female green razorfish

21 CULLODEN

DEPTH RANGE: 23–66 ft (7–20 m)
DIVING EXPERIENCE: Beginner
GPS: N11°14.973 / W060°44.831

The reef lies about 220 yards (200 m) offshore and starts just off one of three large pillars that extend to the surface. The reef slopes steeply to a depth of 66 ft (20 m) where it meets a sandy sea bed and takes on the appearance of fingers of reef separated by sand channels, referred to as a 'spur and groove' reef. The spurs are composed mainly of flat star corals, small brain corals, sea fans, slit-pore sea rods and sea plumes. On the sandy channels, look for the occasional nurse sharks, stingrays and yellowhead jawfish.

Over 50 species of fish are known to inhabit this reef including angelfish, doctorfish, surgeonfish, Spanish hogfish, chromis, grunts, snappers, groupers, wrasse, cardinalfish, gobies, blennies and filefish. Large schools of Creole fish can be seen meandering over the reef, often stopping to feed on the many green algae that cover it.

Juvenile bluehead wrasse foraging for food

22 ENGLISHMAN'S BAY

DEPTH RANGE: 33–83 ft (10–25 m)
DIVING EXPERIENCE: Beginner
GPS: N11°17.823 / W060°40.412

Located on the right of the bay, just off the white, sandy beach, this reef is excellent for both snorkelling and diving. The dive heads north along the edge of this gently sloping reef composed mainly of large boulders and coral heads. Look into the holes, crevices and overhangs formed by the boulders, for lobsters, cardinalfish, fairy basslets, spotted drums and banded coral shrimps. Large schools of Creole wrasse scout the reef in search of food. Cottonwicks often mingle with schooling grunts.

The reef is covered with numerous octocorals including sea rods, sea fans and sea plumes. Stony corals include small brain corals, flatten plate morphyte and mountainous star corals covered with Christmas tree worms.

Christmas tree worms inhabit hard corals

Large schools of cottonwick and yellowtail snapper roam the reef

23 THE SISTERS

DEPTH RANGE: 30–120 ft (9–36 m)
DIVING EXPERIENCE: Advanced
GPS: N11°20.003 / W060°38.714

This group of five large rocks rising from the deep sea bed is divided into two dive sites; the Outer Sisters and the Inner Sisters, each site offering distinct diving.

The **Outer Sisters** is home to some of the largest scalloped hammerheads in Tobago measuring up to 10 ft (3 m) in length though some in excess of 13 ft (4 m) have been seen. The western side of the rocks drops off sharply to the sandy sea bed, and it is most noticeable that the reef here is almost devoid of soft coral. There are small quantities of sea fans, sea rods, brown tube sponges and a variety of sea sprays. However, there are large numbers of Devil's sea whips and wire corals at the deeper end. The massive rocks and boulders that constitute this side of the reef form very large holes and crevices where some of the largest spiny lobsters congregate.

The scalloped hammerheads roam in groups of five to ten, above the large protrusions rising from the seabed. They can be easily approached for photography but, as with most sharks, extreme vigilance and caution is needed. This side of Sisters is one of the few places in Tobago where the elusive mantas are seen feeding in the plankton-enriched waters. Once found in large numbers in the surrounding waters of Tobago, most have now vanished.

The **Inner Sisters** is a complete contrast. There are large varieties of soft corals that include yellow tube sponges, pink vase sponges, barrel sponges, orange ball sponges and several colours of the star encrusting sponge. Large Venus and common sea fans, boulder star corals and numerous varieties of octocorals blanket the reef. Fish life abounds with huge schools of blue and brown chromis, grunts, Creole fish, Creole wrasse, snappers, groupers, parrotfish, angelfish, bigeyes, gobies, blennies, highhats and spotted drums. Occasionally, green turtles and hawksbill turtles are seen. On the sandy edge of the reef look for stingrays, yellowhead jawfish and small snake eels.

Large brown tube sponges

Colourful sponges at Japanese Gardens, Speyside

Man O'War Bay Dive Sites

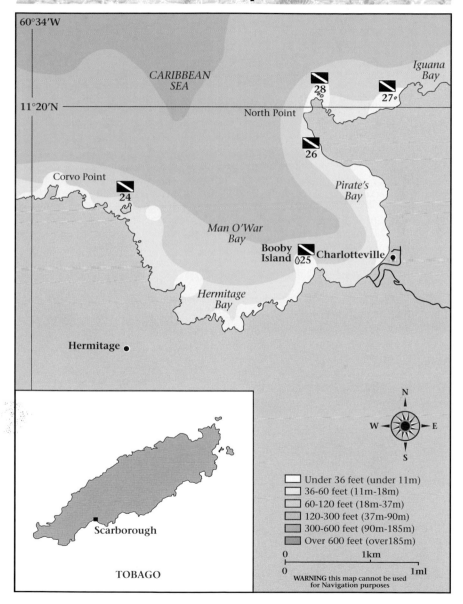

60°34'W

CARIBBEAN
SEA

Iguana
Bay

28

27

11°20'N

North Point

26

Corvo Point

24

Pirate's
Bay

Man O'War
Bay

Booby
Island

25 Charlotteville

Hermitage
Bay

Hermitage

N

W — E

S

Under 36 feet (under 11m)
36-60 feet (11m-18m)
60-120 feet (18m-37m)
120-300 feet (37m-90m)
300-600 feet (90m-185m)
Over 600 feet (over185m)

0   1km
0   1ml

WARNING this map cannot be used
for Navigation purposes

Scarborough

TOBAGO

24 CARDINAL ROCK

DEPTH RANGE: 26–132 ft (8–40 m)
DIVING EXPERIENCE: Intermediate
GPS: N11°19.651 / W060°34.382

Also referred to as Cardinal Sunk, it is located at the western end of Man O'War Bay 164 ft (50 m) from land and is made up of a series of large boulders and vertical walls. The rocky pinnacle extends from 164 ft (50 m) on a sandy sea bed to 10 ft (3 m) above water. The dive starts on the north side of the rock and drops down a vertical wall covered with large sea fans and orange cup coral. Shoals of Creole wrasse and blue chromis are dominant. There is a series of ledges in step-like formation that extends to the base of the pinnacle and which is coated with deepwater sea fans, bipinnate sea plumes large colonies of black corals and encrusting gorgonians.

The dive continues around the rock passing through a sandy channel that is home to yellowhead jawfish and numerous lizardfish. Look under the large overhangs for nurse sharks, turtles and spiny lobsters. Continuing around the southern end, the fish life is prolific with queen angelfish, fairy basslets, snappers and parrotfish. There is an abundance of sergeant majors, Creole fish and black durgon. Depending on the current, the dive can continue west towards land, swimming over smaller pinnacles, or end where the dive started. Either way, this is a very exciting dive with the chance to see large pelagic fish.

Large schools of Creole wrasse are common at Cardinal Rock

25 BOOBY ISLAND

DEPTH RANGE: 16–83 ft (5–25 m)
DIVING EXPERIENCE: Beginner
GPS: N11°11.543 / W060°48.020

Calm, clear water and close proximity to the dive centre make this reef an easy, relaxing dive with a profusion of fish and coral life. The reef around the island is composed mainly of large boulders inhabited by fire coral, small sea fans and encrusting gorgonians and slopes gently to the flat sandy sea bed at 82 ft (25 m). Because of the unusual rock formation, the reef has large holes where spiny lobsters, crabs and chain morays reside. The dive starts on the south-eastern end of the rock near a vertical wall that rises to the surface and continues around the eastern side then heads north. The highlight of this dive is finding the very rare golden hamlet. This species of hamlet is occasionally seen in the eastern and northwest Caribbean but never in the southern areas and Man O'War Bay is the only location where it can be found in Tobago. Look for the shy, reclusive black brotula in cracks and crevices.

The dive continues around to the western side of the island at a depth of 33–50 ft (10–15 m). The huge flat boulders are covered with encrusting sponges, fire coral and small hard and soft corals. There is the usual number of reef fish including parrotfish, groupers, schools of bigeye and angelfish.

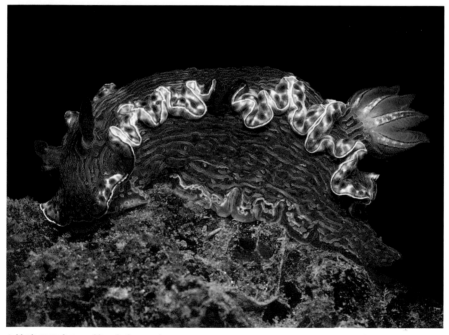

A black-spotted sea goddess feeds on red sponge

26 LANDSLIDE

DEPTH RANGE: 26–50 ft (8–15 m)
DIVING EXPERIENCE: Beginner
GPS: N11°19.910 / W060°33.252

Regarded mainly as a training dive, Landslide is located off the far right of Man O'War Bay and is well protected from waves, surges and currents. Composed of huge rocks and boulders crowned with an extensive variety of hard and soft corals including giant slit-pore sea rods, sea plumes and Venus sea fans, the reef's gentle gradient extends to 50 ft (15 m) where it meets a flat, sandy bed. The prolific marine life, clean, clear water and lack of current are ideal conditions for photography.

The dive heads in a north-westerly direction winding through the numerous boulders. Peacock flounders, southern stingray and large spotted scorpionfish can be found on the sandy patches between coral outcrops. Shoals of chromis, Creole wrasse, grunts and angelfish dominate the reef. Gobies and blennies are plentiful. Look inside basket sponges for banded coral shrimps and small crabs. Landslide makes a particularly good night dive with the chance to see giant basket stars, lobsters and eels.

Colourful sponges and corals at Landslide

27 SANGA ROCK

DEPTH RANGE: 26–100 ft (8–30 m)
DIVING EXPERIENCE: Beginner
GPS: N11°20.368 / W060°32.921

Located at the north point of Man O'War Bay, the dive starts on the eastern side of the rock at 26 ft (8 m). Swimming over the large boulders with a variety of hard and soft corals, takes you around the northern side of Sanga Rock that extends vertically from 115 ft (35 m) to the surface. The wall is covered with a variety of large gorgonians and encrusting sponges. There is an abundance of fish life along the wall including angelfish, wrasses, durgons and small groupers.

Large cracks and crevices are found along the wall that hide fairy basslets, banded coral shrimps and small spiny lobsters. It is possible to circumnavigate the entire rock which will bring you to a sandy beach. However, continuing the dive in a south-westerly direction will take you over a large rubble plain consisting of the large boulders covered with sea fans, giant slit-pore sea rods, sea plumes and a variety of hard corals that make up this reef. The plethora of fish add vivid colour to the reef. Hawksbill turtles are common.

An abundance of fish life and soft corals

28 LONG ROCK

DEPTH RANGE: 16–100 ft (5–30 m)
DIVING EXPERIENCE: Intermediate
GPS: N11°20.156 / W060°33.013

Located 110 yards (100 m) from the northeast end of Sanga Rock, Long Rock extends from 130 ft (40 m) on a sandy bed to 33 ft (10 m) above water. Depending on conditions, the dive can be carried out in two ways. The first starts at 17 ft (5 m) deep and heads in an easterly direction along a steep wall at 100 ft (30 m). An underwater light is useful for looking into the numerous cracks and crevices along the wall that is lightly covered with small sea fans and encrusting sponges. From 60 ft (18 m), looking up to the surface, the waves breaking on the rocks give a dramatic cloud-like appearance that attracts many tarpons. Schools of Atlantic spadefish and ocean triggerfish are a regular sight along the wall.

The second option is a better choice on a rough day. It starts on the eastern side of the rock and heads in a north-easterly direction to 100 ft (30 m) around some large boulder rubble topped with a variety of small hard and soft coral. Fish life includes Queen angelfish, parrotfish and black durgons. Ascending to 50 ft (15 m) the dive then travels west around Long Rock. Look for pelagic jacks, large groupers and cubera snappers along the boulder rubble.

A great barracuda

A Sharknose goby on star coral

St Giles Islands Dive Sites

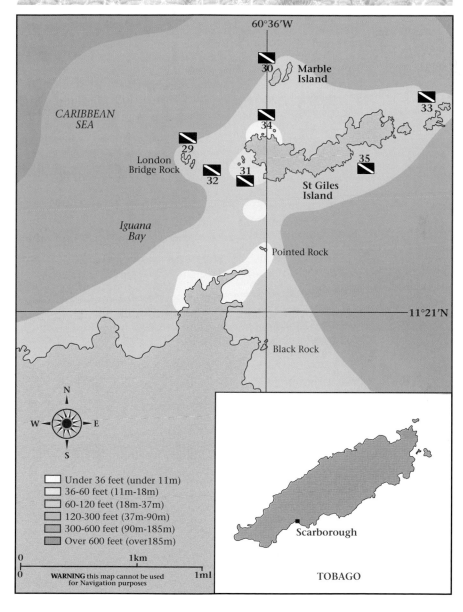

60°36′W

30

Marble
Island

CARIBBEAN
SEA

33

34

29

London
Bridge Rock

32   31

35

St Giles
Island

Iguana
Bay

Pointed Rock

11°21′N

Black Rock

N

W   E

S

☐ Under 36 feet (under 11m)
☐ 36-60 feet (11m-18m)
☐ 60-120 feet (18m-37m)
☐ 120-300 feet (37m-90m)
☐ 300-600 feet (90m-185m)
☐ Over 600 feet (over185m)

0   1km
0   1ml
WARNING this map cannot be used
for Navigation purposes

Scarborough

TOBAGO

29 LONDON BRIDGE

DEPTH RANGE: 40–100 ft (12–30 m)
DIVING EXPERIENCE: Advanced
GPS: N11°21.369 / W060°32.009

The most famous dive in Charlotteville, London Bridge is the largest in a group of three rocks and easily recognisable with its huge, natural arch that extends over water. The highlight of this dive is exploring the passage through the arch but this can only be attempted when surface conditions are good and currents are manageable. The dive can be done in several ways, depending on the current, but normally starts on the northern side at 50 ft (15 m). The reef is made up of massive boulders covered mainly with small gorgonians and encrusting sponges and forms enormous overhangs and crevices where turtles, lobsters and porcupine fish hide. You are guaranteed to see large schools of tarpon along the rocky ridge.

Upon approaching the archway, there are steep walls covered in massive deep-water sea fans, sponges and encrusting gorgonians. Parrotfish, chromis and small shoals of grunts are the main fish here. Wide sand channels with long devil's sea whips and wire coral lead the way to the entrance of the arch that starts at 46 ft (14 m). Divers must enter one at a time as the opening is only 3 ft (1 m) wide and gradually expands to 10 ft (3 m) with the length of the passage being about 100 ft (30 m). If surface conditions are rough, the surge within the passage will be very strong and divers must be negatively buoyant upon entry into the archway and keeping close to the rocky bottom is essential. It is possible to hold on to the rocks at the base for support as it is completely devoid of coral. The highest point within the arch is 33 ft (10 m).

Once through the archway, divers must descend to the sandy bottom at 50 ft (16 m). Depending on the direction of the current, the dive can either continue east where the reef slopes gently or west where the reef drops steeply to a sandy bed at 180 ft (55 m). The coral and fish life on this side of London Bridge is prolific.

London Bridge rock showing archway

30 MARBLE ISLAND

DEPTH RANGE: 33–100 ft (10–30 m)
DIVING EXPERIENCE: Intermediate
GPS: N11°21.760 / W060°31.589

Located 440 yards (400 m) north of the St Giles Island, Marble Island is thought of as one body of land but is actually two separate rocks. The currents caused by the convergence of the Caribbean Sea and Atlantic Ocean, mean that conditions must be ideal for diving to take place safely and local advice should be sought. Depending on the current, the dive can head either north or south. Conditions must be calm in order to pass through the channel between the rock formations. The dive begins outside the rocks at 66 ft

(20 m) then heads in a south-westerly direction following the steep, vertical wall that drops beyond 115 ft (35 m). Coral growth is very sparse.

As the dive continues, heading in a north-easterly direction, the reef flattens out and there are large boulders at the base of the wall, that are completely covered with fire coral, giving them a golden-yellow appearance. On close inspection, small secretary blennies can be found peeping out of empty tube worm burrows.

The reef fish on this side are plentiful. Look for flameback angelfish, palometa, permit, large parrotfish and cubera snappers. Hawksbill turtles, spotted eagle rays and tarpons are just some of the large pelagic life to be found here.

Secretary blennies reside in empty tube worm burrows

31 ROCKY MOUNTAIN

DEPTH RANGE: 20–66 ft (6–20 m)
DIVING EXPERIENCE: Beginner
GPS: N11°21.392 / W060°31.413

This is probably the best protected dive in the area and, therefore, the most frequently visited. Located southwest of St Giles Island, Rocky Mountain presents to the diver, massive coral covered boulders, deep cliffs and wide sandy patches where some of the largest southern stingrays can be found. This dive site also has the largest collection of brain corals and sponges in the area.

The dive starts shallow at 23 ft (7 m) and heads north passing over a large rocky plain. Look within crevices for branching anemones, peppermint shrimps, banded coral shrimps and other invertebrates. Black brotula can be found in deep crevices but lots of patience is required before actually seeing them. This shy cleaner is very reclusive and retreats deep into dark recesses when alarmed. The plate coral overlaps forming deep overhangs where fairy basslets, moray eels, cardinal fish and small spotted lobsters hide. Grunts and cottonwicks congregrate over the reef in large schools.

Several different dives can be executed along this reef all with the same starting point and each offering a different scene.

Shoals of bluestriped grunts hover above giant plate corals

32 OLD ROCKY MOUNTAIN

DEPTH RANGE: 20–66 ft (6–20 m)
DIVING EXPERIENCE: Beginner
GPS: N11°21.790 / W060°32.124

This dive follows the fringing reef that extends from St Giles Island all the way west to London Bridge. After dropping in 33 ft (10 m) and passing over a sandy channel, the dive heads west, soon arriving at a series of large boulders heavily encrusted with sponges, bleeding teeth bryozoans, boulder brain corals stinging bush hydroids and encrusting gorgonians at 66 ft (20 m). There is a profusion of fish life; much more than other dives. Angelfish, black durgons, Creole fish and parrotfish dominate. Nurse sharks can be found on the narrow sandy channels between boulders.

The dive can continue past the boulders towards London Bridge, however, the current tends to increase in strength. The other option is to turn back towards the starting point after passing the boulders. The divemaster usually makes this decision depending on the conditions at that time.

Queen angel roams among a variety of sponges and coral

33 THREE ROCKS

DEPTH RANGE: 33–132 ft (10–40 m)
DIVING EXPERIENCE: Advanced
GPS: N11°22.586 / W060°33.131

Located at the eastern end of St Giles Island is a group of three rocks which, when pounded by the Atlantic Ocean, can only be dived when the surface conditions are very calm and currents are mild or non-existent. This is a dive for advanced and experienced divers. The dive is executed from the furthest rock in the group from either the north or south side of it, depending on the flow of current. After dropping to 33 ft (10 m), the dive heads out towards the point reaching to a depth of 130 ft (40 m).

The sheer drop-off of the wall far beyond 164 ft (50 m) is breathtaking. It is almost vertical all the way to the surface and is covered with a variety of stony corals and encrusting sponges. Green moray eels and tarpons here, are the biggest in Tobago measuring well over 7 ft (2 m) in length. Look for large schools of Atlantic spadefish, jacks and dolphin fish. Huge hawksbill turtles are often spotted swimming along the wall or in open water. Big nurse sharks can be found at the base of the wall in shallow areas.

The rare flameback angelfish is occasionally seen here near the top of the wall. Fairy basslets, queen angelfish, juvenile rock beauty, butterflyfish are just a small sample of the marine life that can be observed along the wall.

Colourful sponges and octocorals adorn this reef

34 WASHAROO

DEPTH RANGE: 33–100 ft (10–30 m)
DIVING EXPERIENCE: Intermediate
GPS: N11°22.885 / W060°35.462

Washaroo is the local name given to the very large midnight parrotfish that is found in abundance on this dive. Located north of St Giles Island, this dive can be done when the northeast trade winds have subsided considerably and the strength of the currents decreased.

The dive heads in an easterly direction at an average depth of 60–70 ft (18–21 m). The reef slopes gently to a sandy bed at 130 ft (40 m) and is covered with huge boulders topped with sea fans, a variety of sponges and hydroids. Along the way there are many 'mini walls' and ample overhangs occupied by nurse sharks, lobsters and squirrelfish. Numerous small caves are scattered along the wall where juvenile spotted drums with their long dorsal fins gather. Look for angelfish, groupers, basslets and other species of parrotfish.

Large barrel sponges are misshapened by the strong currents

35 ST GILES DRIFT

DEPTH RANGE: 33–83 ft (10–25 m)
DIVING EXPERIENCE: Beginner
GPS: N11°22.454 / W060°33.564

On the south coast on the eastern end of St Giles Island is the location of this dive and the reef resembles that of Speyside in many aspects. It is covered with sea plumes, sea rods and sea fans and slopes steeply to a depth of 82 ft (25 m) where it meets a sandy sea bed that has small patches of boulders topped with encrusting sponges and small gorgonians. Because this area experiences strong currents, the dive can travel either east or west but whichever direction, the reef formation is the same.

Look for tarpons, barracudas and turtles above the reef. Large spiny lobsters can often be seen under coral heads on the sandy beds. There is the usual amount of reef fish including hamlets, Creole wrasse, gobies, blennies, filefish and triggerfish. Peacock flounders and southern stingrays are found on the sandy patches.

Shoals of bluestriped grunts hover above giant plate corals

Nassau grouper

The Boulder Brain coral at Speyside is a major tourist attraction

Speyside Dive Sites

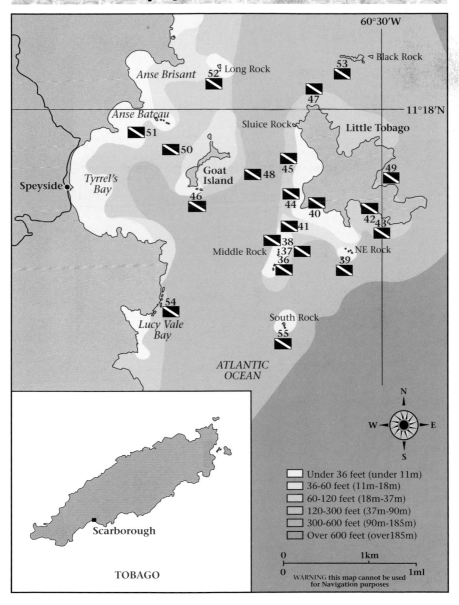

60°30'W

Black Rock

53

Anse Brisant   52 Long Rock

47

Anse Bateau   Sluice Rock   Little Tobago   11°18'N

51

50

Goat   45   49
Island 48

Speyside   Tyrrel's   46   44   40   42 43
Bay   41

38
Middle Rock   37   NE Rock
36   39

54

Lucy Vale   South Rock
Bay   55

ATLANTIC
OCEAN

N
W   E
S

Under 36 feet (under 11m)
36-60 feet (11m-18m)
60-120 feet (18m-37m)
120-300 feet (37m-90m)
300-600 feet (90m-185m)
Over 600 feet (over185m)

0   1km
0   1ml
WARNING this map cannot be used
for Navigation purposes

Scarborough

TOBAGO

36 BOOKENDS

DEPTH RANGE: 30–120 ft (9–36 m)
DIVING EXPERIENCE: Intermediate – Advanced
GPS: N11°17.276 / W060°30.637

The name is derived from the two large rocks with a large vertical gap between them that gives the appearance of bookends. This is one of the more popular dive sites when conditions are good. The dive starts at the western end of the rocks and a negative entry is required because the drop-off point is quite close to the rock where the surge is quite strong. Divers must descend head first as quickly as possible because if they linger on the surface too long there is the possibility of being pushed onto the jagged rocks or drifting into deeper waters. Once down, the reward is the diversity of marine life that includes shoals of grunts, angelfish, parrotfish, Creole wrasse and brown and blue chromis. There are small brain corals and star corals covered with gobies, sea plumes, sea rods, sea fans and the reef is covered with a carpet of serrated strap algae and the green grape algae.

Heading around the northern side of the steep gradient, very large cubera snappers, crevalle jacks, graysby, barred hamlets and queen triggerfish are observed. Where the reef meets the sandy sea bed, there are massive Nassau groupers, long Devil's sea whips and giant barrel sponges. At around 50 ft (15 m),

there is a huge, natural indentation, which is devoid of coral and often referred to as the 'Tarpon Bowl'. Here divers can hover or kneel while looking at the enormous, roaming tarpons or at nurse sharks that lie beneath overhangs. At the shallower end of the dive, the reef is covered with large elkhorn corals that shelter snappers and grunts under their branches, while many passing, blacktip reef sharks can be seen.

One of the many cleaning gobies on a star coral

A diver observes one of the large tarpons at Bookends

37 RUNAWAY

DEPTH RANGE: 30–90 ft (9–27 m)
DIVING EXPERIENCE: Intermediate
GPS: N11°17.350 / W060°30.577

Located 220 yards (200 m) north-east of Bookends, the reef slopes gently to a sandy bottom. The dive travels in a north-easterly direction following the edge of the reef where large spiny lobsters can be seen beneath coral and rocks. The reef is covered by slit-pore sea rods, sea plumes, common sea fans, pillar coral and small brain coral. Almost all of the barrel sponges have been bent out of shape due to the strong currents often present.

Long, streaming schools of Creole wrasse swim constantly over the reef, together with large schools of cottonwick and French grunts. Queen, French and grey angelfish feed on the numerous soft corals.

A wide common sea fan

Nurse sharks can be found lying under the overhangs created by large, honeycomb plate corals. Schools of bigeye often hover in loose associations just above the reef and can be easily approached by divers. Look out for squirrelfish, blackbar soldierfish, scrawled filefish, all varieties of parrotfish and the hundreds of black durgon that roam above the reef.

Caribbean spiny lobsters can grow quite large

38 ALPS

DEPTH RANGE: 50–110 ft (15–33 m)
DIVING EXPERIENCE: Intermediate
GPS: N11°17.368 / W060°30.586

The drop off for this dive is north-east of Bookends. A negative entry is required because of the constant surface current and surge. The Alps probably gets its name because of the rocky reef formation. An extensive variety of hard and soft corals cover the reef, such as fire corals, corky sea fingers, encrusting gorgonians, bent, porous and doughnut sea rods, rough and slimy sea plumes. Sponges consist of the brown tube sponge, branching vase sponge including the fan-shaped greenish-grey variety,

netted and leathery barrel sponge. Most of the Venus and common sea fans are covered by either finger print cyphoma or flamingo tongues. Spanish hogfish, scrawled filefish, shoals of Creole wrasse, French grunts and grey chromis are just some of the residents here.

Midway through this dive at 50 ft (15 m), there is a hole carved in the rock measuring just 4 ft (1.5 m) wide by 20 ft (6 m) long that makes a fantastic swim-through. It is at a 45° angle to the surface. There are spiny lobsters, blackbar soldier fish, broadsaddle cardinal fish and banded coral shrimps within this hole. The dive continues around Bookends and finishes at 50 ft (15 m) in the 'Tarpon Bowl' where huge schools of tarpons hover in the surge at the surface.

A brilliant assortment of corals and sponges

39 TDE SPECIAL

DEPTH RANGE: 30–120 ft (10–40 m)
DIVING EXPERIENCE: Advanced
GPS: N11°17.430 / W060°30.187

Located 985 yards (900 m) from the south-western tip of Little Tobago and 190 yards (175 m) north-east of Bookends, TDE Special is a small group of rocks that can only be dived when conditions are good. The dive begins on the northern face of the rocks, around the southern end and finishes on the north-eastern side. A negative entry is required because of the surge and large waves close to the rocks and the current here can be quite strong at times. This dive is best done at an average depth of 40–50 ft (12–15 m) because it is here that most of the marine life is seen. Divers should avoid venturing too close to the steep walls along the rocks because of the strong surge.

This steeply sloping reef is covered by barrel sponges, large sea fans, small brain coral, sea plumes and a large variety of sea sprays. At the deeper end look for feather black corals and very long Devil's sea whips. There are large tarpons that hang out close to the surface and sometimes venture close to divers. Huge hawksbill turtles can often be seen lying on the reef or sometimes foraging on the soft barrel sponges. Schools of Creole wrasse, Creole fish, French grunts, grey and blue chromis survey the reef together with the occasional barracuda. Very large mutton snappers can be observed on the wall close to the surface. Giant green moray eels peer out beneath the large rocks that make perfect homes for other creatures such as spiny lobsters. Large crevalle and horse-eye jacks swim up to the surface from the deep swirl around divers and then descend back into the deep. It is not uncommon to see eagle rays, nurse sharks and blacktip reef sharks during the dive. True to its name, this is indeed a 'special' dive.

Black corals can often be found very deep at TDE Special

40 CORAL GARDENS

DEPTH RANGE: 30–90 ft (9–27 m)
DIVING EXPERIENCE: Intermediate
GPS: N11°17.599 / W060°30.279

The highlight of this dive is the sight of the largest boulder brain coral in the Caribbean measuring 15 ft (4.5 m) tall and 20 ft (6 m) wide. Coral Gardens is a gently sloping reef located 490 yards (450 m) from the south-western tip of Little Tobago and 55 yards (50 m) from the southern end. The dive begins at 33 ft (10 m) and heads in a north-westerly direction. The reef if covered with a forest of gorgonians, including giant slit-pore sea rods, black sea rods, porous sea rods and large colonies of sea plumes. There are several species of stony corals including starlet coral, maze coral, small boulder brain coral and honeycomb plate coral.

Fish life includes massive schools of French and bluestriped grunts, Creole wrasse and blue and grey chromis. Look for Spanish grunts, porkfish, and black margates under overhangs. At the reef's edge, there are coneys, red hind, black groupers, yellowhead jawfish, turtles and stingrays.

The continuous current makes this a great drift dive, passing large shoals of cottonwick, mutton and cubera snapper. The magnificent brain coral is located towards the end of this dive. Look under it for large, dormant nurse sharks. From here on, the current picks up and heads in a northerly direction passing over very small, yellow tube sponges, sea fans and fire corals while the reef abounds with parrotfish and queen angelfish. Veer left and the dive ends in a calm, shallow bay after passing over a large boulder where nurse sharks seek refuge from the strong current beneath the overhangs. Here peacock flounders, scorpionfish, arrowhead crabs, numerous angelfish, butterflyfish and chubs dominate the reef.

Large barrel sponges at Coral Gardens

The giant boulder brain coral in Tobago is the largest in the Caribbean

41 KELLESTON DRAIN

DEPTH RANGE: 54–120 ft (16–36 m)
DIVING EXPERIENCE: Advanced
GPS: N11°17.564 / W060°30.251

Situated about 330 yards (300 m) from the southern end of Little Tobago and 760 yards (700 m) from Black Jack Hole, the dive starts just at the edge of the sloping reef and heads in a north-westerly direction. This dive also leads to the giant boulder brain coral. The reef is composed mainly of soft corals as well as barrel sponges, giant slit-pore sea rods, spiny sea fans, large sea plumes and small feather black corals at the reef's edge. The current is quite strong and can whisk a diver past large shoals of mutton snappers, Creole fish, black durgon and many species of Caribbean butterfly and angelfish.

Crossing over a sandy patch, the current takes you to another, deeper reef, where huge cubera snapper and Nassau grouper sit idly on the sand. Schools of Atlantic spadefish, horse-eyes and crevalle jacks are seen swimming in the open water above the reef. Look for the numerous scorpionfish, trunkfish, triggerfish and large blue parrotfish. The Devil's sea whips at this end grow to lengths of 8–10 ft (2.5–3 m). The current pushes back to the shallower end where large, slow-swimming barracuda approach divers. Here massive shoals of Caesar and bluestriped grunts can be found above or near the numerous coral formations. The dive ends upon reaching the boulder brain coral.

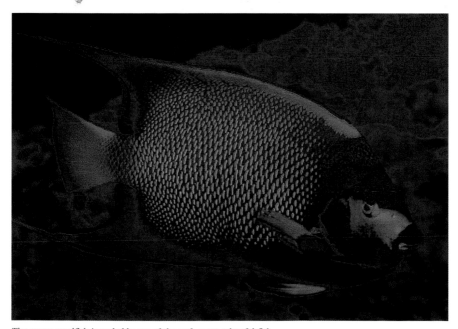

The queen angelfish is probably one of the reefs most colourful fish

42 BLACK JACK HOLE

DEPTH RANGE: 24–132 ft (7–40 m)
DIVING EXPERIENCE: Beginner
GPS: N11°17.648 / W060°29.881

One of several reefs south of Little Tobago, this dive site gets its name from the numerous black jacks that are seen here from May to July. This steeply inclined reef is covered by small brain corals, several varieties of fire coral, black sea rods, slit-pore sea rods, common sea fans and Venus sea fans. Beyond 100 ft (30 m), black coral and Devil's sea whips and wire corals can be found. There are many types of sponges, including large barrel sponge, azure vase sponge and brown and yellow tube sponge. The reef is home to thousands of blue and brown chromis and every known species of Caribbean angelfish including the seldom seen, but very elusive cherubfish that can be found at around 80 ft (25 m).

Large Nassau groupers sit idly at the reef edge moving only upon approach, while black groupers can be seen near the bottom or occasionally in open water well above the reef. Tarpons and great barracuda often approach divers on this dive. Look out for hawksbill turtles, spotted eagle rays, small reef and blacktip sharks at, or near the top of the reef. Large schools of Atlantic spadefish and horse-eye jacks are usually seen at the deeper end of the reef.

Under ledges look for spiny lobsters, green moray eels, squirrelfish, blackbar soldierfish and glasseye snappers. Graysby, red hind, rock hind, coney and several species of snappers are found at the numerous cleaning stations along this reef.

Steeply sloping, colourful reefs are characterisitc of dives in Speyside

43 PICKER

DEPTH RANGE: 50–132 ft (15–40 m)
DIVING EXPERIENCE: Advanced
GPS: N11°17.510 / W060°29.500

On the eastern wall of Little Tobago this dive can only be done when conditions are right. Huge waves and very strong, unpredictable surface and bottom currents make this one of the most challenging dives in Speyside and only experienced advanced divers will be taken. It is done as a negative entry and, if for some reason you cannot make it to the bottom immediately, abort the dive and return to the boat. Those who do get down will be rewarded with the large arrays of pelagic fish. Spotting nurse sharks on this dive is guaranteed as well as a variety of eels, turtles and very large tarpons. This dive site is regarded as the breeding ground for Caribbean spiny lobsters that litter the bottom.

Large barrel sponges, misshapen by the perpetually strong current, make perfect hiding places for small barred hamlets, banded coral shrimps and juvenile yellowtail damselfish. There are many small brain corals, large Venus and sea fans, cup and flower corals and massive starlet corals. It is imperative to stick with the divemaster and not stray on this dive as the current can pull you into deeper water and sometimes the direction of the current can change almost instantly.

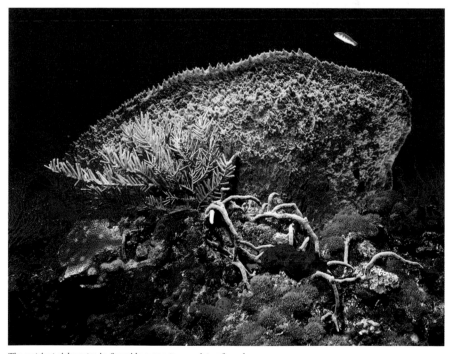

The nutrient-rich water in Speyside supports a variety of corals

44 CATHEDRAL

DEPTH RANGE: 24–90 ft (8–27 m)
DIVING EXPERIENCE: Beginner
GPS: N11°17.757 / W060°30.522

Located just 165 ft (50 m) from the western shore of Little Tobago, the dive begins in just 33 ft (10 m) of water and heads in a north-easterly direction. The Cathedral is at the very end of Kelleston drain and has a steep gradient that ends in a sandy bottom. Large rocks form numerous overhangs where green moray eels, spiny lobsters and the occasional hawksbill turtle hide.

The reef is covered by numerous massive starlet corals, mountainous star corals, giant slit-pore sea rods as well as several sizes and varieties of Venus sea fan. Several sizes of basket sponges are scattered over the reef, making perfect homes for the many banded coral shrimps, arrowhead crabs, bearded fireworms and jewel fish that live here. Fairy basslets can be found in undercuts and small recesses. Large parrotfish, queen, French and grey angelfish, butterflyfish, schools of bigeyes and hogfish can be found in the deeper end of this dive.

The top of the reef is home for thousands of blue and green chromis, French and bluestriped grunts, large schooling chubs and Creole wrasse. Here the reef is covered mainly with elkhorn coral, common sea fans and several large boulder brain coral. Where the reef meets the sand, look for spotted snake eels, yellowhead jawfish and southern stingrays.

Colourful Creole wrasse swim over large brain corals on Cathedral

45 FLYING MANTA

DEPTH RANGE: 50–105 ft (15–35 m)
DIVING EXPERIENCE: Advanced
GPS: N11°17.994 / W060°30.503

This advanced drift dive is located just 330 yards (300 m) from the western shores of Little Tobago and starts where Cathedral ends. The dive heads in a northerly direction and begins on a sandy sea bed. The reef has a steep slope, covered mainly with large branching tube sponges including the yellow and olive varieties, convoluted barrel sponges, branching vase sponges and netted barrel sponges. Octocorals include sea rods, sea plumes and sea fans. This is one of the few dive sites where large mantas might rarely be observed feeding on plankton brought in by the strong currents.

From April to May, it is possible to observe large ocean triggerfish during nesting. They fan a large depression in the sand to lay their eggs and usually swim in loose groups guarding their nests against predators. This reef is one of three sites in Speyside that the seldom seen cherubfish can be found. The large star corals, covered with sharknose gobies, make convenient cleaning stations for the numerous parrotfish, angelfish, coneys, red hinds, mutton snapper and large shoals of French and bluestriped grunts. The corals form very large overhangs and are home to lobsters, arrowhead crabs, blackbar soldierfish, spotted drums and sharptail eels.

During this dive, it is imperative to stick with the divemasters because towards the end of it, the currents can increase in strength, making it very difficult and risky. Divers must pass between a large rock on the left and land on the right, keeping on the shallower end. Outside of this rock, two extremely strong currents travelling in opposite directions meet. This creates a maelstrom that can pull divers into deeper water. The dive ends in a quiet bay where shoals of snapper and chub swim over the myriad elkhorn corals.

A juvenile stoplight parrotfish at a cleaning station

46 JAPANESE GARDENS

DEPTH RANGE: 20–110 ft (6–33 m)
DIVING EXPERIENCE: Intermediate – Advanced
GPS: N11°17.851 / W060°31.148

Situated at the southern end of Goat Island, this site offers another opportunity to see mantas. The drop-off point for this dive is opposite a small rocky ridge. The water is sometimes choppy with a slight surge action so getting down is important. As you make your way down the steeply sloping reef it becomes apparent why this site gets its name. The reef takes on a flower-garden appearance because of the vivid and brightly coloured corals and sponges. Hues of each colour in the rainbow spectrum create a unique richness and vibrancy reflected in the diversity and prolific marine life of this dive site. Small to large, bright yellow tube sponges cover

A brittle star on a lavender row pore rope sponge

Large schools of Creole wrasse add colour to the reef

the reef like a carpet, dotted with the brilliant red sea rods, olive, purple and orange varieties of branching tube sponges and pink vase sponges. The barrel sponges add their shades of grey, brown and red-brown together with rope sponges that come in red, purple and lavender.

The fish life intensifies the colour; the electric blue of the chromis, the purple front to golden rear of the fairy basslet, the queen angelfish's brilliant yellow and blue, the multicoloured stoplight parrotfish and the thousands of Creole fish. The current is mild at the beginning of the dive but picks up midway. At a steady 50 ft (15 m) several large boulders with a natural split measuring 7 ft (2 m) across, will come into view. Divers must enter this 10 ft (3 m)-long passage known, as 'Kamakazee Cut' in single file, as missing it will result in being pulled into deeper waters. Once through to the other side, the current slows down considerably and, on rare occasions, is non-existent. Expect to be greeted by a plethora of Creole wrasse while gigantic tarpons swim freely in the deep and barracudas hover, often bold enough to approach divers. The reef then slopes steeply and numerous reef boulders are covered mainly with small brain corals, large sea fans speckled with flamingo tongues, tube sponges, fire corals, giant slit-pore sea rods, sea plumes and branching vase sponges. Beneath the overhangs look for sleeping nurse sharks, lobsters and spotted moray eels.

Clean, clear blue water, healthy reefs and a wide variety of fish makes Japanese Gardens a photographer's dream

47 ANITA

DEPTH RANGE: 36–90 ft (11–27 m)
DIVING EXPERIENCE: Beginner
GPS: N11°18.470 / W060°30.384

Located in a calm bay on the northern tip of Little Tobago, this dive begins on a very flat, sparsely covered, sandy sea bed where queen conch exist in large quantities. Look for the occasional manta at the surface as well as hawksbill turtles. The dive continues around the point heading in a south-westerly direction. The reef slopes steeply to the surface and is covered by large, coral-covered boulders that form small caves where graysby, blackbar soldierfish and glasseye snapper hide.

Several large barracudas patrol the reef and often approach divers. Many large cubera snapper can be seen darting around the reef. At the deeper end of the dive, among the large barrel sponges, look for massive schools of grunts and cottonwick. Large spiny lobsters can be seen peering out from under the small coral heads or under rocks. On the sandy sea bed, look for small southern stingrays and yellowhead jawfish.

Divers exploring one the the many steep slopes at Anita

48 OUTER SPACE

DEPTH RANGE: 20–100 ft (6–30 m)
DIVING EXPERIENCE: Advanced
GPS: N11°18.281 / W060°30.290

At 164 ft (50 m) to the left of Flying Manta, this deep, advanced drift dive rewards divers with large pelagic jacks such as horse-eye, crevalle and almaco. Heading in a northerly direction, the reef is teaming with both hard and soft corals including feather black coral, large barrel sponges, long stove pipe sponges and huge colonies of sea plumes and sea rods. Below the mountainous star coral look for nurse sharks, sleeping hawksbill turtles and large spiny lobsters. There are large shoals of grunts, cottonwick, parrotfish and bigeyes.

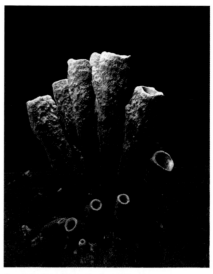

Exquisite formation of yellow tube sponge

Juvenile bluehead wrasse meander around fire coral

49 GRAND CANYON

DEPTH RANGE: 40–110 ft (12–33 m)
DIVING EXPERIENCE: Intermediate – Advanced
GPS: N11°17.978 / W060°29.861

Located on the eastern end of Little Tobago where the sheer rocky cliffs rise vertically from the sea floor, Grand Canyon can only be dived when conditions are favourable since large waves can cause strong surge currents. The water is usually quite clear along this exposed wall, which increases the visual splendour of the dive. Along the wall you will find many different sponge species including the yellow tube sponge, brown tube sponge, netted barrel sponge, row pore rope sponge and encrusting sponge. There is a wide variety of corals such as

giant slit-pore sea rods, spiny sea fans, common sea fans, colourful sea rods and sea whips.

This exposed side of the Atlantic Ocean is fed by a continuous flow of nutrient-rich water, attracting an array of fish life. It is the abode to some of the largest midnight parrotfish, blue parrotfish and groupers. Large hawksbill turtles and smaller green turtles are often seen here gliding over the reef in search of food. Look for blacktip reef sharks and small schools of eagle rays as they dart in and out of the reef.

At the shallower end of this dive, large schools of blue and brown chromis, Creole wrasse and French grunt are abundant. Crevalle jacks and horse-eye jacks are often spotted in the open water.

Secretary blenny in star coral

50 ANGEL REEF

DEPTH RANGE: 15–60 ft (4–18 m)
DIVING EXPERIENCE: Beginner
GPS: N 11°18.059 / W060°31.530

This is a great dive site for novices because of the depth range, but advanced divers will also find this site exciting. Located just off the western side of Goat Island, this fringing reef is an essential visit for photographers looking for a variety of coral and fish life. Although this dive site is located midway between the mainland and Goat Island, the visibility is usually good throughout the year and the current tends to be quite gentle. The dive follows a north-easterly direction.

The corals and sponges at Angel Reef are very healthy despite the battering the reef endures during the hurricane season. Large barrel sponges are prominent as well as a variety of corals including the finger coral, mountainous boulder star coral, brain coral, great star coral, massive starlet coral, honeycomb plate coral, colonies of sea plumes, black sea rods and bent sea rods.

Huge schools of Creolefish, chromis and Creole wrasse dominate the reef. Look under coral heads and ledges for large spiny lobsters, green moray eels, squirrelfish and the occasional nurse shark. Small blacktip reef sharks regularly roam in search of a meal. Look at the sandy edge of the reef for stingrays and electric rays as well as large Nassau groupers, black groupers and mutton snappers. There are numerous cleaning stations scattered along the reef, enabling many great photo opportunities for snapping sharknose gobies, scarlet-striped cleaning shrimps and Pedersen cleaning shrimps as they pick parasites off angelfish, parrotfish, groupers, and snappers.

Boulder brain coral at Angel Reef

Angel reef is often the choice for night dives because of the wide variety of marine life that inhabit it and the short boat ride to the site. Giant basket stars, often closed during the day, extend their long arms at night to feed on plankton. Shine your dive light and observe the glowing eyes of the thousands of red night shrimps that roam the reef. Other night creatures to look for include spotted scorpionfish, anemones, eels, toadfish and parrotfish wrapped in a protective cocoon while they sleep. Dived either by day or night, Angel Reef makes for a fascinating and truly enjoyable dive.

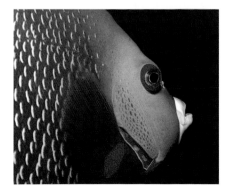

French angel fish

51 AQUARIUM

DEPTH RANGE: 40–70 ft (12–21 m)
DIVING EXPERIENCE: Intermediate – Advanced
GPS: N11°18.283 / W060°31.437

Located just off the point in Bateau Bay and south of Brisant Bay the reef extends from the mainland to a group of rocks jutting out of the water known as Weather Rocks. This dive can only be done when the seas are calm because huge waves and surge prevent boats from approaching the site.

The dive begins south of Weather Rock and usually heads in an easterly direction around the rocks then north. The drop-off here is quite deep and the current is often strong. As the name implies, this site is truly an aquarium with an abundance of coral and fish life. Corals consist of yellow and brown tube sponges, leathery barrel sponges, scattered pore rope sponges and numerous encrusting sponges. There is a huge variety of hard and soft corals including slit-pore sea rods, spiny sea fans, common and Venus sea fans, boulder brain corals and cup corals.

Expect to see enormous schools of Creole wrasse, chromis and grunts. Hawksbill and green turtles are common on this site as well as nurse sharks and southern stingrays. Peer under ledges for giant green morays and spiny lobsters. Large barracudas are often spotted patrolling the reef, inquisitively approaching and following divers around the reef. Look for schooling tarpons, southern sennets, bogas and other pelagic fish.

Diver examines a large barrel sponge

52 JOHN ROCK

DEPTH RANGE: 20–90 ft (6–27 m)
DIVING EXPERIENCE: Advanced
GPS: N11°18.632 / W060°31.099

Also known as Long Rock, this dive site is located just outside Brisant Bay and can only be dived when conditions are optimal since large waves and surge can make this dive impossible. Although this site is not often dived, when conditions are favourable, divers will be richly rewarded with sightings of numerous, large pelagic fish. The dive begins on the south side of the rocks, heading west and around to the northern point. The site drops off steeply, almost vertically and the current here can be quite strong sometimes so it is important to keep as close as possible to the slope, especially when bull sharks approach. It is imperative to watch the

divemaster since the current is unpredictable and can change direction of flow in an instant.

Although the area here has sparse coral growth, the sponges are abundant due to the prolific flow of plankton and include stove-pipe sponges, yellow tube sponges, brown bowl sponges and an assortment of rope sponges.

Upon entry into the water, huge bull sharks often emerge from the deep and make a close pass then they rapidly descend to the deep. Some often hang around longer and make great photo opportunities. Bull sharks are considered dangerous but are wary and move away when approached. Reef sharks and blacktip sharks are also seen here along with other pelagic fish including tarpons and barracudas.

Secretary blenny in pink sponge

53 SLEEPER

DEPTH RANGE: 35–85 ft (11–26 m)
DIVING EXPERIENCE: Advanced
GPS: N11°18.860 / W060°30.220

Similar to John Rock, this dive site is totally dependent upon weather conditions and is located north of Little Tobago at a site called Black Rocks. This set of rocks is exposed to very strong currents and winds, making Sleeper a dive site that is seldom visited. When the conditions are favourable, the dive begins south of the rocks where the slope is gentle and heads east and, if the currents are not too strong, it is possible to dive the northern side where the slope is more vertical.

The coral and sponge growth near the surface is quite sparse due to the pounding of the waves on the rocks. Avoid diving near the surface where the surge and white water are more severe. Deeper down the slope, look for branching vase sponges, encrusting sponges and scattered pore rope sponge. There are more hard corals consisting mainly of maze corals, smooth star corals and fragile saucer corals.

There is a good chance of seeing blacktip reef sharks and the occasional bull sharks. Look for tarpons, barracudas and the occasional eagle ray. A variety of parrotfish inhabit this reef including the very large midnight parrotfish. Large black groupers are often seen drifting in open water or at the numerous cleaning stations.

On the northern side of the rocks the slope drops off dramatically to the deep and here the surge and currents are worse if conditions change. There are less sponges and corals than on the southern side but the fish life here abounds. Massive schools of southern sennets, boga and Atlantic spadefish are seen in the open water. There is a wide variety of damselfish, snappers, and parrotfish.

Juvenile burrfish

54 SPINY COLONY

DEPTH RANGE: 15–90 ft (5–27 m)
DIVE EXPERIENCE: Beginner
GPS: N11° 16.270/W060°32.020

Located just north of Lucy Vale Bay and along the side of a steeply sloping cliff, this dive site is a good option for both beginner and advanced divers offering an array of corals, sponges and fish life. The dive heads north along the edge of the cliff and meanders around large coral heads and boulders towards Tyrell's Bay.

Avoid diving near the cliff as the surge here is quite strong. Look under the numerous coral heads and overhangs for spiny lobsters, eels, fairy basslets and a

multitude of various blennies and gobies. Peacock flounders are perfectly camouflaged against the sandy seabed. Goat fish and the occasional flying gurnard can be observed foraging for shrimp and other shellfish in the sand. Hawksbill turtles, a favourite subject of photographers, can be seen resting on the sand or feeding on different types of sponges.

As the dive continues north the coral heads are smaller and further apart. Here, nurse sharks are found sleeping near these corals and provide many excellent photo opportunities. Towards the end of the dive it is advisable to swim out to the open ocean, away from the cliffs and surge since it is easier for the boat to pick up divers.

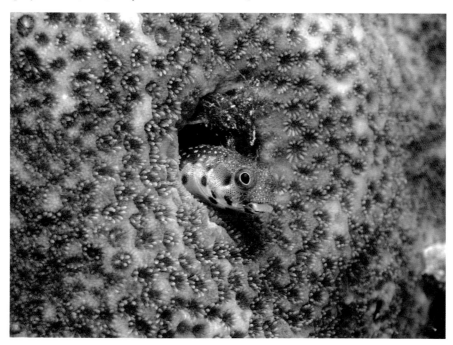

A secretary blenny peers out of a star coral

55 SHARK BANK

DEPTH RANGE: 30–90 ft (9–27 m)
DIVE EXPERIENCE: Advanced
GPS: N10°15.695 / W060°30.628

Also known as South Rock, this dive site is located east of Lucy Vale Bay and south of Little Tobago Island. It is exposed to rough waves and strong currents that make it quite difficult to navigate. Avoid the upper water column as the surge and white water make diving impossible. The dive starts on the southern end of the rock and heads in a clockwise direction following the flow of current but, because the dive conditions here are unpredictable and can change quite rapidly, the dive will sometimes head in an anti-clockwise direction. Because of the unpredictable nature of the current it is imperative to keep an eye on the divemaster and follow his lead.

There is an abundance of sponges and corals consisting mainly of barrel sponges, rope sponges, encrusting sponges, sea fans, knobby sea rods, spiny sea fans and various sea plumes.

As the name implies, there is a good chance of seeing nurse sharks and blacktip sharks as well as other large pelagic fishes. Hawksbill turtles, tarpons and barracudas are regular sightings on this dive along with the colourful presence of parrotfish, damselfish, blennies, gobies, snappers and groupers.

Front view of a sand diver

MARINE IDENTIFICATION GUIDE

This marine identification guide presents a small sample of the diverse life found in the waters of Trinidad and Tobago. Scientific names are provided for divers with an interest in taxonomy.

Reef butterflyfish
Chaetodon sedentarius

Longsnout butterflyfish
Chaetodon aculeatus

Foureye butterflyfish
Chaetodon capistratus

Blackbar soldierfish
Myripristis jacobus

Bluehead wrasse
Thalassoma bifasciatum

Blue Tang juvenile
Acanthurus coeruleus

Bluestriped grunt
Haemulon sciurus

Bridled goby
Coryphopterus glaucofraenum

Sharknose goby
Gobiosoma evelynae

Coney
Cephalopholis fulvus

Cottonwick
Haemulon melanurum

Honeycomb cowfish
Acanthostracion polygonia

Barred hamlet
Hypoplectrus puella

Graysby
Cephalopholis cruentatus

Bigeye
Priacanthus arenatus

French angelfish
Pomacanthus paru

Queen angelfish
Holacanthus ciliaris

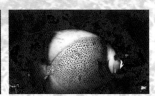
Gray angelfish
Pomacanthus arcuatus

Harlequin bass
Serranus tigrinus

Princess parrotfish
Scarus taeniopterus

Stoplight parrotfish juvenile
Sparisoma viride

Sharpnose puffer
Canthigaster rostrata

Peacock flounder
Bothus lunatus

Porcupinefish
Diodon hystrix

Highhat
Pareques acuminatus

Brown chromis
Chromis multilineata

Blue chromis
Chromis cyanea

Green razorfish
Xyrichtys splendens

Doctorfish
Acanthurus chirurgus

Rock beauty
Holacanthus tricolor

Sand diver
Synodus intermedius

Smooth trunkfish juvenile
Lactophrys triqueter

Spotted drum
Equetus punctatus

Squirrelfish
Holocentrus adscensionis

Whitespotted filefish
Cantherhines macrocerus

Bicolor damselfish
Stegastes partitus

Yellowtail damselfish
Microspathodon chrysurus

Threespot damselfsh juvenile
Stegastes planifrons

Longfin damselfish juvenile
Stegastes diencaeus

Spotted scorpionfish
Scorpaena plumieri

Green moray
Gymnothorax funebris

Purplemouth moray
Gymnothorax vicinus

Banded coral shrimp
Stenopus hispidus

Rough fileclam
Lima scabra

Bearded fireworm
Hermodice carunculata

Corkscrew anemone
Bartholomea annulata

Florida corallimorph
Ricordea florida

White encrusting zoanthid
Palythoa caribaeorum

Five-toothed sea cucumber
Actinopygia agassizii

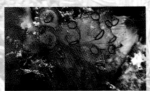
Bulb tunicate
Clavelina sp.

Slate-pencil urchin
Eucidaris tribuloides

Yellow tube sponge
Aplysina fistularis

Orange lumpy encrusting sponge
Ulosa ruetzleri

Star encrusting sponge
Halisarca sp.

Boulder brain coral
Colpophyllia natans

Split-crown feather duster
Anamobaea orstedii

Social feather duster
Bispira brunnea

GLOSSARY

Technical

Benthic Of the bottom of the sea and the marine life that dwells or roams there, e.g. nurse sharks, jawfish, blennies.

Coral Marine animals living in colonies that build complex marine ecosystems. They belong to phylum Cnidaria, class Anthozoa and include hard (stony) and soft (gorgonian) corals. Hard corals create skeletal formations of calcium carbonate from seawater, working in symbiosis with zooxanthellae and are the reef-builders.

Corallimorph Marine animal of class Anthozoa, often confused with sea anemones, but recognised by a flat body with concentric rings of short, knob-like, radial tentacles, surrounding a protruding mouth at the centre.

Echinoderm Group of animals belonging to phylum Echinodermata, having five body sections of equal size, arranged around a central axis, e.g. crinoids, sea stars, brittle and basket stars.

Mantle A specialised covering over the body of molluscs that is responsible for shell formation in certain snails. Often very colourful with intricate patterns and can extend over the shell as a form of camouflage, mimicry or defence, e.g. flamingo tongue or on the body of shell-less snails, e.g. nudibranchs.

Mollusc Group of soft-bodied animals belonging to phylum Mollusca, consisting of snails, shell-less snails, chitons, squid, octopuses, bivalves.

Nematocyst Stinging capsules attached to tentacles of animals in phylum Cnidaria.

Nudibranch Shell-less, marine snail of class Gastropoda, with vibrantly colourful mantles.

Pelagic Of the open ocean and freely moving marine animals, e.g. mantas, hammerhead sharks, barracudas, whales.

Pirogue Type of diving or fishing boat of a particular design, common to Trinidad and Tobago. Has characteristic low stern with high bow.

Polyp Individual coral animal body unit that attaches itself to a substrate where it will spend the rest of its life reproducing, and building coral colonies with millions of polyps. Each polyp has a ring of tentacles surrounding a single body opening, the mouth.

Prostomium Structure that holds the whorl-like radioles in Christmas tree worms.

Radiole Feather-like appendages attached to the prostomium of Christmas tree worms or to the hard tube of feather duster worms. They cover a relatively large surface area that enables dual functionality of catching food and allowing oxygen uptake from seawater.

Segmented worms Also known as Polychaetes, they belong to phylum Annelida and include fireworms, Sabellids (feather duster worms) and Serpullids (calcareous tube worms, e.g. Christmas tree worms.)

Sponge Simple, multicellular animals of phylum Porifera. There are many variations in shape, size and colour.

Symbiosis A close association of animals and plants of different species that is often, but not always mutually beneficial.

Thermocline Layer of cold water, more common in Trinidad waters than Tobago.

Tunicate Very small, colourful, translucent animals belonging to subphylum Urochordata, often mistaken for sponges as they also attach to a substrate, but are much more developed with nervous, digestive, reproductive and circulatory systems.

Urochordata A subphylum of Chordata. Animals that have no backbone but showed the required characteristics of vertebrate classification, at some point in their development.

Zoanthid Often confused with anemones, although in same class Anthozoa. Smaller and distinguished by two rings of tentacles around the oral disk compared with a single ring in anemones.

Zooxanthellae Marine algae that live within the tissue of coral polyps; essential to the survival of reef-builiding corals through a delicately balanced, symbiotic relationship.

Ethnic Food

Bake A fried quick bread used as a complement to buljol or fried shark, also known as 'floats'. Baked recipe variants include 'Coconut bake' and 'Johnny bake'.

Benne balls Hard confection of sesame seeds in caramelised sugar, shaped into balls, more common in Tobago.

Black cake Very dark coloured, moist, soft-textured fruitcake made at Christmas time or as wedding cakes. The fruits (prunes, cherries, raisins) are soaked for an extended period in cherry brandy or other alcoholic spirits before use.

Black pudding Concoction of pig's blood and spices encased in intestinal lining. It looks like a large, black sausage but is not. Best eaten with hops bread and pepper sauce.

Buljol Shredded, cooked, salted codfish (hake or pollock) sautéed in olive oil with onions, tomato and black pepper. It is best eaten with bake or hops bread.

Calalloo Green soup made with okra, pumpkin, coconut milk and 'calalloo bush' or leaves of the dasheen (taro) plant. It can be eaten as an appetizer or an entrée with crabs.

Chadonbenni (culantro) Indigenous, aromatic herb (*Eryngium foetidum*) often confused with cilantro but unrelated though similar, with flavour that is more robust. Also called 'shado benny' and used in cooking or in hot sauces and chutneys.

Channa Common ingredient of Indian food usually curried and eaten with roti and is the main ingredient in Doubles filling. Also called garbanzo beans or chick peas.

Chutney Saucy, peppery Indian condiment usually made with tamarinds, mangoes or other innovations with local fruits. Best eaten with Indian finger foods like phoulorie, kachourie, saheena or biganee.

Coconut milk/water The milk is a white liquid extracted from the minced pulp of hard, dry coconuts. It is used more as an ingredient in cooking as in calalloo, pelau or oil down. Coconut water is a clear liquid, freshly available from green coconuts as a naturally sweet drink, rich in electrolytes. It is also an excellent mixer for Scotch.

Coo coo Dish based on cornmeal with carrots and okra. Caribbean version of polenta.

Dasheen (taro) Root tuber and type of blue food or ground provision.

Doubles Indian 'fast food' made with a curried channa mixture, sandwiched between two soft, fried pieces of dough, called bara. Often dressed with hot sauce or chutneys.

Ginger beer Slightly fermented ginger drink often served at Christmas time.

Hops bread Type of local bread with a characteristic hard, crumbly crust.

Kuchela Indian condiment of shredded, dried mangoes in mustard oil with seasonings.

Mauby (mabi) Bittersweet local drink made from boiled bark of the soldierwood tree (*Colubrina elliptica*), flavoured with aniseed.

Oil down Dish of boiled breadfruit in coconut milk.

Pelau Rice dish with pigeon peas and stewed pieces of chicken or beef.

Pastelles Type of tamale made with cormeal dough filled with a ground beef or chicken mixture of chopped olives, capers and raisins and wrapped in banana leaves.

Plantain Large banana species that requires cooking before consumption.

Pone Sweet, sticky pie of grated coconut and cassava (manioc).

Roti Soft Indian flatbread eaten on the side with accompaniments or wrapped with curried fillings. Local types are sada, paratha or 'bus' up shot' and dhaalpourie.

Sea moss Milky health drink made from extracted gel of certain species of seaweed.

Sorrel (roselle) Dark red drink made from floral relative to the hibiscus family (*Hibiscus sabdariffa*), flavoured with cloves and cinnamon. Commercially available year round but also freshly made in many homes at Christmas time. Not in any way related to the sorrel (*Rumex* sp.) used in salad greens.

Souse Boiled snout, ears or tail of pig in a clear sauce flavoured with hot peppers, lime, cucumber and onions. Served at room temperature or cold.

DIVE CENTRES

ADVENTURE ECO-DIVERS LTD. (PADI Resort)
Le Grand Courland,
Black Rock, Tobago.
Tel: 868 639 8729
Fax: 868 639 3993
Email: ecodiver@tstt.net.tt
Boats: 1 pirogue, covered.

AQUAMARINE DIVE (PADI Gold Palm Resort)
Blue Waters Inn
Speyside, Tobago
Phone: 868 660 5445
Fax: 868 639 4416
Email: amdtobago@trinidad.net
Website: www.aquamarinedive.com
Boats: 3 pirogues, covered

EXTRA DIVERS TOBAGO (PADI Resort)
Pigeon Point Road
Crown Point, Tobago
Tel/Fax: 868 639 7424
Email: extradivers@tstt.net.tt
Website: www.extra-divers.de
Boats: 2 pirogues, uncovered. Offers
PADI, NAUI and TDI courses.

FRONTIER DIVERS LTD.
Sandy Point Beach Club,
Crown Point, Tobago.
Tel: 868 631 8138
Mobile: 868 683 7210
Website: www.frontierdiverstt.com
Email: dougdives@tstt.net.tt
Boats: 1 pirogue, covered.

MANTA DIVE CENTER (PADI Resort)
P.O. Box 1090,
Bon Accord, Tobago.
Location: Pigeon Point
Tel/Fax: 868 639 9969/639 9209
Mobile: 868 678 3979
Email: mantaray@tstt.net.tt
Website: www.mantadive.com
Boats: 1 pirogue, uncovered; 1 large dive
boat, covered.

M-DIVE
Main Road,
Speyside, Tobago
Tel: 868 660 6117
Mobile: 868 780 4769
Email: redmanm_dive@yahoo.com
Boats: 1 pirogue.

R & SEA DIVERS (PADI Resort)
Spence's Terrace
Milford Road,
Crown Point, Tobago
Tel/Fax: 868 639 8120
Email: rsdivers@tstt.net.tt
Website: www.rsdivers.com
        www.rsea.de
Boats: 1 pirogue, uncovered.

SCUBA ADVENTURE SAFARI (PADI Resort)
Pigeon Point Road,
Crown Point, Tobago
Tel: 868 660 7767
Fax: 868 660 7333
Email: info@divetobago.com
Website: www.divetobago.com
Boats: 1 Island Hopper, covered.

SUBLIME SCUBA
Tropikist Hotel
Tel: 868 639 8512
Website: www.sublimescuba.com
Email: sublime@tstt.net.tt
Boats: 1 pirogue, covered.

TOBAGO DIVE EXPERIENCE
P.O. Box 115
Scarborough, Tobago
Location: Speyside
Phone: 868 639 7034 or
        800 544 7631 in the US
Fax: 868 660 5030
Email: info@tobagodiveexperince.com
Website: www.tobagodiveexperience.com
Boats: 3 pirogues, all uncovered. Offers
PADI, NAUI and BSAC courses.

UNDERSEA TOBAGO (PADI Resort)
Coco Reef Resort
Store Bay, Tobago
Tel: 868 631 COCO (2626)
Fax: 868 639 7759
Email: undersea@tstt.net.tt
Website: www.underseatobago.com
Boats: 2 covered.

WILD TURTLE DIVE SAFARI (PADI Resort)
Club Pigeon Point,
Pigeon Point, Tobago
Tel: 868 639 7939
Fax: 868 635 1011
Email: info@wildturtledive.com
Website: www.wildturtledive.com
Boats: 1 pirogue, covered.

WORLD OF WATERSPORTS
(PADI Gold Palm Resort)
Tobago Hilton
Lowlands, Tobago
Tel: 868 660 7234 (PADI)
Fax: 868 660 8326 (TEAM)
Email: info@worldofwatersports.com
Website: www.worldofwatersports.com
Boats: 1 pirogue, covered.

TRINIDAD
Private tours and tuition available from
the author, Solomon Baksh
Email: solobaksh@gmail.com

OVERNIGHT DIVE SAFARI
Manta Dive Center (See listing above)
Boat: Viking IV – meals prepared on
board, fresh water shower, toilet
facilities, limited sleeping
accommodation. Overnight trips from
Pigeon Point to Speyside, Charlotteville,
St Giles Islands.

LUXURY LIVE ABOARD
PETER HUGHES DIVING, INC.
5723 NW 158 St. Miami Lakes,
FL 33014, USA.
Tel: 305 669 9391
Toll free: 800 9 DANCER
Fax: 305 669 9475
Email: dancer@peterhughes.com
Website: www.peterhughes.com
Boat: MV *Wind Dancer*, 120ft.
Accommodates 18 divers.

CONTACT INFORMATION

Tourism and Industrial Development Company of Trinidad and Tobago Limited (TIDCO)
10–14 Philipps Street,
Port of Spain, Trinidad
Tel: 868 623 1932/4
Fax: 868 623 3848
Website: www.visitTNT.com

Unit 12, IDC Mall, Sangster's Hill,
Scarborough, Tobago
Tel: 868 639 4333
Fax: 868 639 4514

Tobago House of Assembly
Department of Tourism, Transportation,
Enterprise Development and Settlement
Doretta's Court, 197 Mt Marie,
Scarborough, Tobago
Tel: 868 639 2125
Fax: 868 639 3566
Website: www.visittobago.gov.tt
Email: tourtobago@tstt.net.tt

Association of Tobago Dive Operators (ATDO)
Website:www.tobagoscubadiving.com
Email: ecodiver@tstt.net.tt
Tel: 868 639 8729

Chaguaramas Development Authority
Carenage, Trinidad
Tel: 868 634 4227/ 4364
Website: www.chagdev.com
Email: chagdev@tstt.net.tt

Asa Wright Nature Center & Lodge
Arima Valley, Trinidad.
Tel: 868 667 4655
Fax: 868 667 4540
Email: asawright@tstt.net.tt

In the USA: Caligo Ventures Inc.
Toll Free: 800 426 7781
Email: Margaret@caligo.com

Pointe-à-Pierre Wildfowl Trust
Pointe-à-Pierre, Trinidad.
Tel: 868 658 4210 or 4200 Ext.2512
Tel/Fax: 868 628 4145
Website: www.trinwetlands.org
Email: wildfowl.trust@petrotrin.com

Nature Seekers (Turtle Guides)
Matura, Trinidad.
Tel: 868 668 7337

Trinidad & Tobago Field Naturalists Club
Tel: 868 632 4852

HOTELS AND GUEST HOUSES

TOBAGO

Arnos Vale Hotel
Arnos Vale
Tel: 868 639 2881/2
Fax: 868 639 4629
Website: www.arnosvalehotel.com

Bananaquit Apartments
Store Bay Local Road
Tel: 868 639 9733

Belleviste Apartments
Sandy Point
Tel/Fax: 868 639 9351
Website: www.trinidad.net/belleviste

Blue Haven Hotel and Shutters on the Bay
Bacolet
Tel: 868 660 7400
Fax: 868 660 7900
Website: www.bluehavenhotel.com

Blue Waters Inn
Speyside
Tel: 868 660 BLUE (2583)
Fax: 868 660 5195
Website: www.bluewatersinn.com

Coco Reef Resort and Spa
Crown Point
Tel: 868 639 8571
Fax: 868 639 8574
Website: www.cocoreef.com

Cuffie River Nature Retreat
Runnemede
Tel: 868 660 0505
Fax: 868 660 0606
Website: www.cuffie-river.com

Grafton Beach Resort
Black Rock
Tel: 868 639 0191

Fax: 868 639 0030
Website: www.grafton-resort.com

Hampden Inn
Lowlands
Tel/Fax: 868 639 7522
Website: www.seetobago.com/tobago/
resorts/hampden

Hilton Tobago
Lowlands
Tel: 868 660 8500
Fax: 868 660 8503
Website: www.hilton.com

The Hummingbird
Store Bay Local Road
Tel: 868 635 0241

Johnston Apartments
Store Bay
Tel: 868 639 8915
Website: www.johnston-apts.com

Manta Lodge
Speyside
Tel: 868 660 5268
Fax: 868 660 5030
Website: www.mantalodge.com

Mount Irvine Bay Hotel and Golf Club
Mt Irvine Bay
Tel: 868 639 8871
Fax: 868 639 8800
Website: www.mtirvine.com

Sherwood Park Apartments
Carnbee
Tel: 868 639 7151, 660 8038

Stone Haven Villas
Black Rock
Tel: 868 639 0361
Fax: 868 639 2604

Sunshine Holiday Apartments
Bon Accord
Tel: 868 639 7482
Fax: 868 639 7495

The Palms Villa Resort
Signal Hill
Tel: 868 635 1010
Fax: 868 635 1011
Website: www.thepalmstobago.com

Toucan Inn and Bonkers
Store Bay Local Road
Tel: 868 639 7173
Fax: 868 639 8933
Website: www.toucan-inn.com

TRINIDAD

Hilton Trinidad and Conference Center
Port of Spain
Tel: 868 624 3211
Fax: 868 624 4485
Website: www.hilton.com

Kapok Hotel
St Clair
Tel: 868 622 5765
Fax: 868 622 9677
Website: www.kapokhotel.com

Coral Cove Marina Hotel
Chaguaramas
Tel: 868 634 2040
Fax: 868 634 2248
Website: www.coralcovemarina.com

Crews Inn Hotel and Yachting Center
Chaguaramas
Tel: 868 634 4384
Fax: 868 634 4542
Website: www.crewsinn.com

Mt Plaisir Estate Hotel
Grande Riviere
Tel: 868 670 8381
Fax: 868 670 0057
Website: www.mtplaisir.com

Power Boats Mutual Facilities Ltd
Chaguaramas
Tel: 868 634 4303
Fax: 868 634 4327

The Bight Hotel and Restaurant
Chaguaramas
Tel: 868 634 4427
Fax: 868 634

Crowne Plaza
Port of Spain
Tel: 868 625 3361-8
Fax: 868 625 4166
Website: www.crowneplaza.co.tt

Courtyard by Marriott
Port of Spain
Tel: 868 627 5555
Fax: 868 627 6317
Website: www.marriott.com

Ambassador
Port of Spain
Tel: 868 628 9000
Fax: 868 628 7411
Website: www.ambassadortt.com

The Chancellor
Port of Spain
Tel: 868 623 0883
Website: www.thechancellor.com

INDEX

Page numbers in *italic* indicate illustrations.